The

Gnomes™

Book

HARRY N. ABRAMS, INC., PUBLISHERS, NEW YORK

of

Christmas Crafts

Carol Endler Sterbenz

Library of Congress Cataloging in Publication Data
Sterbenz, Carol Endler.
   The gnomes book of Christmas crafts.

   Includes index.
   SUMMARY: Step-by-step instructions with
patterns and diagrams for more than 50 gnome
inspired Christmas decorations and crafts.
   1. Christmas decorations. 2. Handicraft.
I. Title.
TT900.C4S73 745.59 80-14245
ISBN 0-8109-0967-7 (HNA)
ISBN 0-8109-0968-5 (Special)

Library of Congress Catalog Card Number: 80-14245

Inspired by *Gnomes* by Rien Poortvliet and
Wil Huygen © 1976 Unieboek B.V./Van Holkema
& Warendorf, Bussum, The Netherlands

English translation © 1977 Unieboek, B.V.

Text © 1980 Carol Endler Sterbenz

Published in 1980 by Harry N. Abrams, Incorporated,
New York

Printed and bound in the United States

Technical Writer
LINDA MACHO

Project Director
LENA TABORI

Photographer
MARK KOZLOWSKI

Editor
MARYA DALRYMPLE

Technical Artist
JANET AIELLO

Designer
JOHN S. LYNCH

Script & Handwriting
DIANE LYNCH

*Thanks go to Laura Ashley, NYC, for the loan of the women's and children's clothing;
L.L. Bean, Freeport, ME, for the men's clothing;
F.A.O. Schwarz, NYC, for the toys under the tree;
Liberty Bell Christmas Inc., NYC, for the wreaths and decorative apples;
American Tree and Wreath, NYC, for the garland;
Radiant Decorative Lights, NYC, for the candle lights.*

Contents

For my wonderful children,
Genevieve, Rodney, and Gabrielle.
And especially
for my husband, John,
dream-tender, the best person
in the whole world

Acknowledgments

Having lived so long with the dream of writing a book, I now find it impossible to name the many persons whose influence and help have made it a reality. However, there are some to whom I am especially grateful: my mother, whose love, *sisu* (to use a Finnish word), and teaching equipped my hands and heart to express my dream; my father, whose philosophy of life and belief in me inspired my quest; and my sisters, Nancy and Joan, whose perspective and friendship supported me throughout.

And although it seems as if I have been writing this book forever, it was written this past year—perhaps the longest and shortest of my life. That such a loving group of friends and advisors should come together at this precise time remains a puzzlement, one of the many magical coincidences with which this project was filled. I want to thank Margaret Gilman, Managing Editor of *McCall's Needlework & Crafts* Magazine, for her early encouragement; Lena Tabori, who recognized and sustained me; Marya Dalrymple, my editor, for her enthusiasm and guidance; and Nai Chang and John Lynch, whose spirit and gift for creating miracles brought everything together.

Throughout the project I was assisted by several apprentices with special skills, who added life to my designs: Janet Aiello, technical artist; Linda Macho, technical writer; Donata Delulio, sewing; Dennis Gai, wooden toys; Pearl Gittleson, pottery; Annie Guenot, sewing and appliqué; Nancy K. Johnson, ceramics; Yvonne Johnston, woodcarving; Mary Sassone, stained glass; and Joan Spira, cooking and needlepoint.

On location in Hurley, New York, we were made completely welcome by Carolyn and Stephen Waligursky, who offered their beautiful eighteenth-century home, the Patentee Manor (where Stephen reproduces seventeenth- and eighteenth-century lighting fixtures), for eight days of photography. Their warmth and hospitality are deeply appreciated.

For their participation as carolers, the Johnson, Morehouse, and Greene children deserve thanks for braving the cold.

And I offer my special thanks to Mark Kozlowski, the photographer, to his assistants, Bob Willis and Bo Hopkins, and to his stylist, Elaine O'Donnell—their patience and help made a difficult task achievable.

Introduction

In my attic workroom, there is just enough space for a bed and a worktable by the window that overlooks the bay. Attached to the table top on the righthand side is a white metal bin with a spring lid, which holds some sewing supplies—needles, pins, scissors, odds and ends. I leave the lid open so I can reach things easily, but a careless nudge can trip the spring and clamp one's hand painfully between bin and lid.

The hours spent in this room are particularly long around Christmas as I prepare my crafts for the customers who come looking for handmade things. One Christmas Eve, after the children had been coaxed to bed, I stayed late at my table, trying to finish some little gnome dolls that I had promised them. These were the very last projects I had to do, and I seemed to be getting nowhere.

I examined the little gnome doll in my hand; his body was perfect—sturdy of leg, stout of belly, with his strong hands clasped behind his back.

But something was not quite right about his face. I had failed to capture his whimsy, his wise melancholy. . . . This gnome looked a little stupid. I had seen a real gnome once, but that memory was too hazy a reference to be of any use now. I began gathering little folds around the gnome doll's eyes and, with a stitch or two more, puckered his determined mouth. I was met with the same stupid expression.

Outside it was so dark that I could see nothing but a few splinters of light radiating from the distant shore. My eyelids began to droop. As daybreak was still several hours away, I lay down on top of the bedcovers, thinking that after a short nap I might work better. But fatigue robbed me of sleep. Suddenly a moving blur of red caught my attention. Two little gnomes in tall pointed caps were scooting across the floor. In a moment they had hoisted themselves to the top of my worktable.

Wide awake now, I sat up to get a closer look—but they jumped down off the table and disappeared between the molding and the floorboards. I went over to the spot and ran my fingers along the molding. As if by magic, a small section shifted aside, revealing a tiny doorway opening onto what appeared to be a narrow staircase that fell steeply into the darkness below. Surely this was a passageway into the gnomes' home—right here in my own house!

Since childhood I had felt a kinship with gnomes. Around Christmastime especially, the little *tomte* were included in our traditional family festivities like eccentric relatives, ancestors from the Old Country. We regarded them seriously, for it was an accepted fact that gnomes could be quite mischievous if not well treated. Though our gnomes never made it to the dinner table, my sisters and I felt we knew an astonishing amount about them. In the evenings, Father would describe the sweet, warm smell of the hay in the old barn in Denmark and the steaming porridge that he always set out for the gnomes on Christmas Eve. When he got to the part where the gnomes would come out of hiding, Father would talk in a near whisper and we would all hug our knees and shiver with excitement....

The faint aroma of baking bread escaping through the tiny doorway at my feet brought my thoughts back to the present. I paused a moment, then slid the section of molding back into place. If I hoped to see the little visitors again, I must not keep peering into their home. I went back to work, stitching and pinching the same little face, but it still wasn't right. My brief glimpse of the gnomes had certainly not helped my work. Overwhelmed by frustration and fatigue, I let my head fall on my folded arms and fell asleep.

Perhaps half an hour or so later, I sensed a presence in the room with me and opened my eyes. Just inches from my elbow were the same two gnomes. The smaller of the two was holding my doll, while the other appraised it. Digging his heels into the table, the taller gnome tightened a loose thread in the doll's head. He stood back, cocked his head from side to side, and looked at his companion. Then he reached forward and this time pinched the doll's nose until it was turned up slightly. Extraordinary! He had achieved in a moment what I had not been able to do all night.

Almost as one, the two gnomes turned and stared at me. But before I could say a word, the smaller gnome dropped the doll, stepped back, and accidentally slipped onto the edge of the supply bin. To my horror the spring lid snapped shut, trapping the gnome inside. Only a portion of his red cap stuck out. The other gnome stood motionless at first, then jumped quickly off the table, tumbling over and over till he came to rest sprawled out against the wall. Righting himself, he vanished through the doorway in the molding.

Surely the trapped gnome must have thought himself done for. I opened the bin slowly and his red cap dropped to the bottom. He crouched nearby, looking more embarrassed than frightened.

"Hand me my cap," he ordered with surprising authority.

I reached down and handed it to him with two fingers. The gnome immediately put it on, but then pulled it off with a grumble, kicking the bin wall as he did so.

"This will never do. This cap is torn. It needs mending," he said gruffly, pointing to a large, jagged tear in the front. "Get me something for my head while you're fixing it."

"What unusual manners you have," I said indignantly, as I reached for his cap. He looked down and pulled at his beard.

"Sorry, but you've not caught me at my best," he apologized. "I feel lost without my cap."

I grabbed a scrap of flowered fabric and tossed it into the bin. He tied it under his chin like a kerchief, then asked for a lift out. I set him down on the worktable, where he made himself comfortable on a stack of patterns; but it was only after I had closed the bin lid that he really relaxed and began to speak.

"My name is Timme, and I must say this is all quite unexpected. Torben and I were on our way to collect the porridge that your children had set out when we decided to come up here and look around. We had been told about your workroom by a friend who once needed a needle for medical purposes. You see, a mother fox had gotten a thorn in her foot and was suffering....Our friend was led here by the kind Mr. Forsström who tends your garden. Anyway, I'm afraid our detour has turned into a mess...."

"I feel so responsible for your trouble," I said sincerely.

"You're in a sorry fix yourself, you know," Timme responded. "Your work isn't done and your children will be up soon." He paused thoughtfully, crossing his legs and tugging at his beard, and then continued. "Sewing is really not my province, but you've helped me and I intend to repay you. From now on I will come back as often as I can to help you at your work." I continued making hurried stitches in his cap. "But don't start relying on me too much," he added, "for if word gets out that I am in the homely arts, I will certainly be laughed at...." Timme then pulled a tiny pair of scissors from his pocket. He snipped some thread and then deftly guided it through one of my small needles. Quickly he sewed little laugh wrinkles around the gnome doll's eyes and held it up for my inspection.

Just then a burst of giggling erupted from the narrow doorway, where there were now five gnomes. Two were falling on top of each other as they howled with laughter. Timme's face, framed by the flowered kerchief, reddened.

"That's quite enough," said a serious voice. The laughter stopped, and a very distinguished-looking gnome approached from the rear of the group. "Timme, your friend Torben here told us of the great danger you were in. Other than your lack of cap, however, you seem quite intact." By now the gnomes had gathered around Timme and were teasing him about his temporary headgear.

"I'm all right now," he said, as he pulled off the kerchief and pulled on the mended cap. A few giggles more escaped from the others.

"I can explain," I offered haltingly. They looked at me and settled down to listen as I recounted the events of the evening in detail. After that we continued to talk in excited bursts, each of us interrupting with impatient questions until the horizon began to glow. Soon the bay became a great mirror for the brightening sky. Quickly, the gnomes took their leave. Timme was the last. He waved and called "*Slitzweitz*," then slid the molding back into place and was gone.

I sat very still for a while and watched the sun light up Christmas Day. I realized that the evening had left me with much more than a lifelike gnome doll. For in entering an unknown realm, suspended somewhere between my childhood and the present, I knew I had discovered the true meaning of Christmas.

It is in the spirit of that encounter that I offer this book, for without Timme these special projects might never have been completed. As you work on each of them, your personal touch will reflect not only your own creativity, but your family traditions as well. Start off with the craft project that inspires you most, taking your level of competence into consideration (the complexity of each craft has been indicated). In some cases the designs strongly suggest a particular use; however, you may want to adapt the crafts to your own home-decorating or gift-giving needs. For instance, all the soft-sculpture crafts could be used as toys or as *objets d'art*. Where applicable, suggestions for adaptations are included at the end of the craft directions. You may also want to apply a craft technique different from the one that is originally indicated. For example, most of the painted designs can be embroidered *or* appliquéd.

Feel free to experiment, and you will be rewarded by the results. Don't worry about your finished project not looking exactly like the picture in the book. Irregularities are an expected and charming part of all handmade crafts.

And encourage your children to get involved (especially in the kitchen, where you can eat your mistakes if you want to). Long after their little hands have lost their chubbiness, your creations will be precious heirlooms—remembrances of Christmases past.

—Carol Endler Sterbenz

Glossary

Appliqué: A separate piece of fabric that can be hand- or machine-sewn or glued onto a background fabric as a decorative motif.

Backstitching: Strengthening the beginning and end of a seam by making several stitches forward and backward along the seamline.

Basting: Temporary stitches (about ¼″ long and ¼″ apart) done by hand or machine for a variety of purposes, e.g., to hold fabrics together; to gather an edge.

Bisque firing (also known as biscuit firing): Firing ware that has not been glazed as a final process, or firing ware to facilitate handling in the glazing process.

Blocking: Straightening a worked needlepoint canvas by tacking it to a wood surface over marked guidelines, then wetting the piece with water. When the piece dries, the canvas should be straight and can then be framed.

Breaking pliers: Tongs used for applying breaking pressure along straight scores when cutting stained glass pieces.

Burnisher: A wooden tool with a rounded end used to press down the edges of copper foil on stained glass; an orange stick can be substituted.

Calipers: A tool with two curved hinged legs used for measuring the inside or outside diameter of pottery.

Casing: A channel of fabric through which an elastic or drawstring is pulled.

Cone: A three-sided ceramic pyramid that will bend at a specific temperature in a kiln to record the progress of the work done by the heat.

Coping saw: A hand-held saw used for cutting curves and straight sections of wood.

Copper foil: An adhesive-backed strip of copper used to cover the cut edges of stained glass before applying solder.

Cramp: A tool used to hold work while it is being carved, or to hold glued pieces tightly together until the glue dries.

Facing: A second piece of fabric used to finish and conceal a raw edge. A facing is stitched to the original fabric with right sides together and raw edges even, then turned to the wrong side and pressed, making a smooth, finished edge.

Florist's pick: A wooden stick with one pointed end used to support and attach flowers, leaves, and vegetation to a base.

Flux: A liquid or paste formula used to prepare a copper-foiled or leaded surface for soldering; it cleans the surface and enables the solder to take hold.

Fusible webbing: A fabric of heat-sensitive fibers. If sandwiched between two fabrics and pressed with

a hot iron, it will fuse them together; also adds stiffness and some strength to the fused fabrics.

Glass cutter: A tool with a notched handle and steel wheel used for cutting stained glass; must be held perpendicular to the glass when cutting.

Grozing pliers: Flat, wide-nosed pliers used to snap off pieces of stained glass too small to grasp by hand; also used to break off, or "groze," any tiny chips on the edges of the glass.

Jig saw: A stationary saw that allows for interior and exterior sawing of curved, scrolled, or straight sections of wood; portable model also available.

Leather hard: The condition of partially dried clay when shrinkage has stopped and the surface has not become lighter in color; ware is still soft enough to turn or finish, yet firm enough to handle without fear of distortion.

Lining: A second piece of fabric that is sewn to a garment or needlework project to cover inner construction details, prevent stretching, and preserve the shape of the piece.

Overglaze: A final finish put on pottery.

Patchwork: Needlework consisting of two or more pieces of fabric sewn together to make a larger fabric.

Piping: Covered cord trim.

Porcelain clay: A mechanically strong blend of materials that will become translucent upon bisque firing; the glaze on porcelain is usually fired at a very high temperature, making the piece hard and resistant to abrasion.

Quilting: Hand- or machine-sewing through two or more layers of lightly padded fabric in a design or pattern to produce a raised effect.

Raffia: A strong, flexible, tan-colored natural fiber that can be dyed in almost any shade.

Rapidograph pen: A technical fountain pen that uses India ink; available in point widths from very fine (0000) to thick (9). Number 1 suggested.

Reduction kiln: A furnace or oven with a limited supply of oxygen used to fire clay; clay and glaze are robbed of part of their oxygen content during firing, causing color and surface changes.

Rice grass: Decorative dried grass of the rice plant.

Run: A break in a score on stained glass.

Seam allowance: The distance from the sewing line to the edge of the fabric (¼" for most projects).

Slip: A suspension of clay or glaze in water; indispensible for throwing, attaching pieces, and repairing cracks.

Sloyd knife: A heavy backboned knife used in block carving.

Soft sculpture: A fabric work stuffed with batting or fiberfill that can be transformed into a three-dimensional shape through stitching.

Solder: Any of various fusible alloys (usually 60% tin/40% lead, or 50/50) used to join copper-foiled edges or lead joints together.

Soldering iron: An electrical tool used to apply solder to stained glass; heats up readily and maintains its temperature for a long time to melt the solder.

Stencil brush: A brush with a blunt end usually made of hogs' hair; available in a variety of sizes.

Stencil paper: Semi-transparent white waxed paper that is water resistant, easy to cut, and withstands rough handling; use .005 thickness. Acetate can also be used for stencils and is durable and washable; primarily used for repetitive stencil designs.

Tack cloth: Cheesecloth dipped in varnish to make a sticky cloth used to pick up particles of sanded wood before painting or varnishing; will also clean away particles of sanded varnish.

Template: A guide used for drawing repetitive shapes, usually made from sturdy cardboard (coat edges of cardboard with clear nail polish).

Throwing: Forming plastic clay into different shapes (usually hollow) using the momentum of the potter's wheel.

Throw off a hump: A method of throwing small shapes from one cone of clay using the momentum of the potter's wheel.

Topstitching: Stitching above or below a seam on the right side of the fabric through all thicknesses.

Trimming needle: A large needle used to remove excess clay from the main body of a ceramic piece.

Underglaze: A decoration painted on clay that is either unfired or bisque fired; later it is covered with a transparent overglaze.

Wedging: Kneading and cutting clay to eliminate air and make it homogeneous and plastic.

General Directions

HOW TO ENLARGE PATTERNS

Each pattern to be enlarged is bordered by a grid of squares. Connect lines of grid horizontally and vertically using colored pencil for contrast; entire pattern is now blocked off in squares. Draw same number of squares on large sheet of paper, making each square the size indicated on outer grid of pattern. Working block by block, draw lines of design in each square, enlarging lines to fit into larger squares. Retrace enlarged pattern, strengthening and straightening lines where necessary.

WOODWORKING

MATERIALS: Sharp pencils. Cork-backed steel ruler. Masking tape. T- or carpenter's square. Carbon paper. Jig or coping saw. Medium and fine sandpaper. Tack cloth. Waterproof glue. *For crafts requiring painting:* Small tubes Artists' oil colors: Cadmium Red Medium, Ultramarine Blue, Cadmium Yellow Medium, Vandyke Brown, Flesh, Black, White (or as in individual craft directions). Nos. 2 and 6 sable hair brushes. Turpentine. Marine spar varnish. *For carving stopcuts:* ⅜" straight firmer chisel. ⅝" No. 5 straight gouge. ⅜" No. 7 straight gouge. Mallet or small block of wood. Cramp. Scrap wood or cardboard. *See individual craft directions for additional materials.*

Enlarge patterns if necessary following directions above. Using a very sharp pencil and carbon paper held in place with masking tape, transfer pattern outlines to wood. Mark pattern pieces on wood with longest dimensions along grain; also mark curved edges along grain if possible. Use jig or coping saw to cut out pieces along marked lines as directed. Sand cut edges with medium, then fine, sandpaper until smooth.

For figures, cut with jig or coping saw. Sand front and back of piece until smooth, always sanding with grain. When figures have been carved, smooth rough edges with fine sandpaper, but do not smooth away chisel marks, which are part of the design. Dust pieces carefully with tack cloth.

For carving, cramp work to bench using scrap wood or cardboard between work and cramp to prevent bruising wood. To carve letters, make stopcuts as follows: Using ⅜" straight firmer chisel, cut center line down middle of each letter to depth of about ⅛"; use mallet or block of wood to hit top of handle. Starting from outside of letter, chisel down toward bottom of stopcut, first from one side, then from the other. This will form a "V"-shaped channel (*see Stopcut Diagram*).

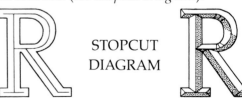

STOPCUT
DIAGRAM

Paint or stain piece as directed for individual crafts; allow to dry thoroughly. Complete any other details necessary for each individual project, then give piece two or three coats of varnish back and front, unless otherwise directed. Allow to dry thoroughly between coats. Lightly sand smooth between coats with very fine sandpaper for a super-smooth finish.

SEWING

MATERIALS: *See individual crafts*

Most patterns and measurements include a ¼"
seam allowance, indicated on patterns by areas
beyond dash lines. Bracketed arrows pointing to
seam indicate that that seam should be placed on
fold. Solid line indicates hem line. Trace or enlarge
patterns as directed, then pin to suggested fabrics,
and cut out along seamlines. Transfer dots, X's, or
other markings to wrong side of fabric; transfer all
appliqué placement or embroidery lines to right
side of fabric as follows: Center pattern over fabric
with a piece of graphite paper in between and pin;
trace pattern with tracing wheel, hard lead pencil,
or dry ball-point pen. Remove pattern and tracing
paper. When following measurements for pieces
without patterns, mark lines or circles on fabric
using ruler or compass, and cut out along marked
lines; these measurements will always include a ¼"
seam allowance. If fabrics ravel, zigzag-stitch, or
pink raw edges with pinking shears.

Complete all embroidery and appliqué designs
before sewing pieces together, unless otherwise
directed. To sew, set stitch length on sewing machine for 10 to 12 stitches per inch. For basting, set
stitch length for 6 to 8 stitches per inch. Sew two
pieces together with right sides facing and raw
edges even, making ¼" seams. Secure stitches by
backstitching at beginning and end of each seam. If
possible, always press seam allowances open. Clip
into seam allowances at curves to ease stress.

For hand sewing, slip-stitch or whip-stitch with
small invisible stitches using matching thread.

a master pattern out of thin, stiff cardboard; coat
edges of cardboard with clear nail polish to prevent fraying and let dry. Place cardboard pattern
on wrong side of fabric and trace around it with
sharp pencil. Remove and mark a second line ¼"
beyond the marked line for seam allowance (unless pattern already includes seam allowance).
Continue to mark suggested number of pieces in
this way, making sure you allow for a ¼" seam
allowance when positioning cardboard for marking. Cut out backing fabric following individual
directions; mark entire appliqué design on right
side of fabric for placement. When sewing, use
matching thread.

HAND APPLIQUÉ
Having marked pattern pieces, machine-sew along
original design outline (*see Diagram A*). Cut out
along marked seam allowance line. Clip into seam
allowance at curves to facilitate turning, then press
seam allowance to wrong side (*see Diagram B*). Pin
appliqué to background fabric and slip-stitch in
place (*see Diagram C*).

MACHINE APPLIQUÉ
Having marked pattern pieces, cut out along seam
allowance line. Pin, then baste pieces to background fabric without turning under edges. Machine-sew pieces to background along original
design outline; trim away any excess fabric to ⅛"
from machine stitching (*see Diagram D*). Set sewing
machine for close zigzag satin stitch. Sew around
each appliqué, covering straight stitches and excess fabric (*see Diagram E*).

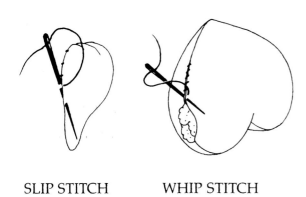

SLIP STITCH   WHIP STITCH

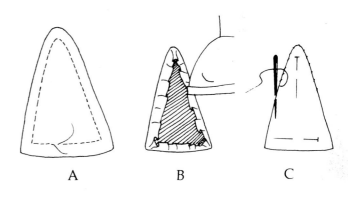

A   B   C

HAND APPLIQUÉ

APPLIQUÉ

MATERIALS: *See individual crafts*

Work with firm, closely woven fabrics to avoid
unnecessary raveling. Trace or enlarge each separate appliqué pattern as directed, pin to suggested
fabric, and mark around outline on fabric using
sharp pencil. (*Note:* Appliqué patterns in this book
do not include seam allowance unless indicated in
directions.) If individual craft directions require
cutting out many appliqués of the same shape, cut

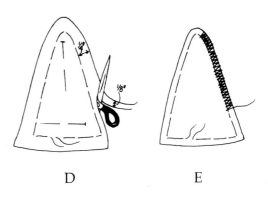

D   E

MACHINE APPLIQUÉ

EMBROIDERY

MATERIALS: *See individual crafts*

Trace embroidery pattern. Transfer design to right side of fabric as follows: Place fabric right side up on work surface. Place a piece of graphite paper over fabric, then center pattern over fabric and paper. Pin. Trace around all design lines, using a hard lead pencil or dry ball-point pen. Remove pattern and graphite paper. Do not cut out design until after embroidery is complete, unless otherwise directed.

Stretch area to be embroidered in embroidery hoop to hold fabric taut; reposition hoop as necessary, and pull fabric taut in hoop if it begins to sag while working. Embroider design following individual directions, Color Key, and Stitch Details.

Begin embroidering by leaving end of floss on back of fabric and stitching over it to secure; do not make knots. To end a strand or begin a new one, weave the floss under stitching on back. If floss begins to kink or twist while you are embroidering, allow needle and floss to hang straight down to unwind.

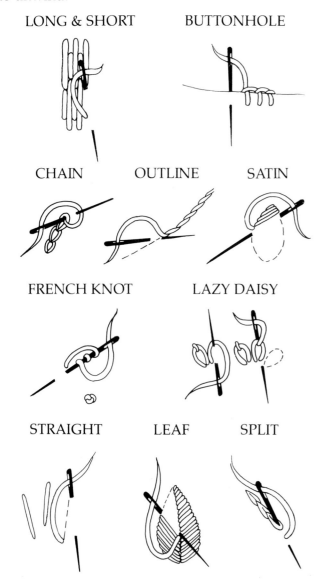

LONG & SHORT BUTTONHOLE

CHAIN OUTLINE SATIN

FRENCH KNOT LAZY DAISY

STRAIGHT LEAF SPLIT

When embroidery is complete, steam press on padded surface.

MACHINE EMBROIDERY

Soft fabrics may require a backing (like tissue paper) to prevent stitches from puckering fabric. Pin backing to wrong side of fabric just under area to be worked. For random stitch machine embroidery, set sewing machine to straight stitch, stitch length to 12, and pressure to darn. With area to be worked under lowered presser foot, begin stitching slowly, guiding fabric in a back and forth motion, stitching "W's" or parallel lines as desired.

For satin stitch machine embroidery, set sewing machine to zigzag stitch, stitch length to 25 or finer, and pressure to normal. With area to be worked under lowered presser foot, begin stitching slowly, following design to be embroidered or filling in area as desired.

SOFT SCULPTURE HEAD

MATERIALS: *See individual crafts*

Cut circle of fabric from muslin following individual directions for size. Hand-baste around circle, 1" from raw edges, using strong thread. Gently gather perimeter of circle, forming pouch. Fill center of pouch with fiberfill until stuffed to medium firmness. Pull basting tight and adjust gathers of muslin ball evenly, concentrating major gathers on one side of ball, which will later be the back of head. Tie off thread. Using pencil, lightly mark positions for eyes, nose, and mouth on upper half of ball of muslin; features will appear to be high.

Cut out nose from muslin, using pattern in individual directions. Gather bottom of nose and stuff gathered portion with fiberfill (*see Diagrams A and B*). Then lightly stuff upper portion of nose. Secure fiberfill inside nose with cross stitches (*see Diagram C*); do not pull thread too tightly or close the opening. Slip-stitch nose to marked position on face (*see Diagram D*).

To form nostrils and bulbous portion of nose, work each side separately as follows: Pinch top and bottom of one side of nose between thumb and index finger. Secure pinched area with four or five tiny stitches; start stitches from underneath nose where nostril will be, running needle through fiberfill toward side of nose. Stitch toward middle of nose and be sure to pull thread tightly between stitches (*see Diagram E*). Secure.

To form bridge of nose, start thread from inside of one nostril and come out on one side of bridge. Run stitches behind bridge, from one side to the other, until length of bridge is pinched and folded (*see Diagram F*). The nose is one of the gnome's most distinguishing features, so take your time and don't get discouraged. And don't worry if your stitches show; they will later be covered with paint. Let the diagrams and photos guide you.

To form eyelids, pinch a narrow fold of fabric and fiberfill over each eye. Curve fold slightly, running tiny stitches through it to secure fabric and fiberfill (*see Diagram G*). To set off lower part of eye, make small running stitches through fabric and fiberfill, pulling stitches taut to form indentations. Some laugh or squint wrinkles will form as you do so—these are desired. (*Note:* For closed eyes, such as those on the Female Gnome Tea Cozy, page 146, make running stitches for closed eyelid, following drawing and photograph.)

To form cheeks, work each side separately. Pinch a fold on an angle from nose toward jaw. Secure

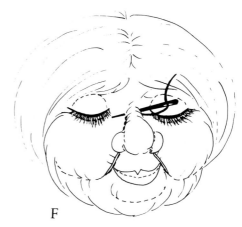

F

NOSE & CHEEK STITCH DIAGRAM

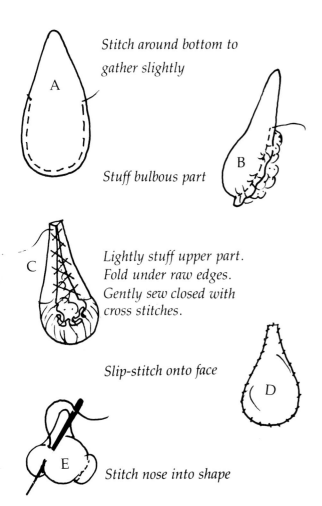

Stitch around bottom to gather slightly

A

Stuff bulbous part

B

C

Lightly stuff upper part. Fold under raw edges. Gently sew closed with cross stitches.

Slip-stitch onto face

D

E

Stitch nose into shape

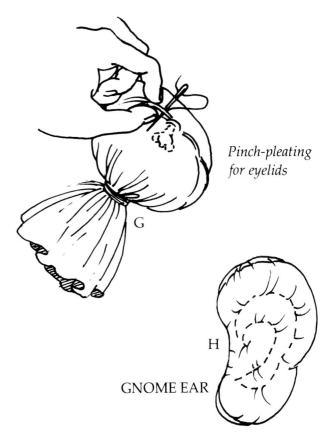

Pinch-pleating for eyelids

G

H

GNOME EAR

fold with running stitches, ending just below mouth line. Continue stitches, curving upward, to form bottom of cheek, while simultaneously working fiberfill upward to puff cheek (*see Diagram F*). Try to make second cheek same size as first. Delineate mouth with tiny running stitches curving upward. Give the female gnome a double chin of tiny running stitches and additional wrinkles as shown in *Diagram F* and photographs (the lower portion of the male gnome's face is covered by his beard).

To form the male gnome's ears (the female's are covered), cut two small circles from muslin following individual directions for size. Make running stitches close to raw edges of circle and draw fabric up, making pouch. Fill pouch with fiberfill and flatten, with raw edges centered on one side (this will be side that gets sewn to head). Following *Diagram H*, make tiny running stitches through fabric layers and fiberfill to make convolutions in ears. When satisfied with ears, stitch to head.

PAINTING
Make flesh-colored acrylic paint using a dab of white paint in cup of water; add small dabs of red and yellow, and mix well. Paint entire head evenly except for eyes. While face is still wet, dilute dab of red paint in another cup of water and apply to cheeks, nostrils, and tips of ears; let red bleed into fabric. If bleeding does not occur, dip brush in plain water and brush around cheeks, blending red into flesh evenly. Paint eyeballs white, as directions indicate. When dry, mix blue paint with steel gray and dab on for irises. Paint white or light gray highlight at left top corner of each iris. Mix dabs of burnt sienna and pink, and dilute with water. Paint lips. Dilute sienna/pink mixture even more, and use to paint wrinkles on forehead, chin, and around eyes. For eyelashes and fine wrinkle lines below eyes, use brown felt-tipped fine line marking pen; test it on scrap fabric to make sure brown doesn't bleed.

19

HAIR

When satisfied with head, set aside and prepare wig. For female, using appropriate wig pattern found with individual directions, cut one pattern as is, and one reverse pattern, from white fake fur, with nap going down. Fur must have a nap of at least 1½ to 2". Do not cut through fur, but do cut through the backing, then separate strands carefully. Sew wig pieces together along marked seamline, which becomes the "part." Brush hair toward back and make bun. For male, curve strip of fake fur to fit around back of head between ears; cut and glue in place. Cut beard using pattern given in individual directions; glue to face. Cut additional tufts of fake fur for moustache and sideburns. For both male and female gnomes, cut small eyebrows from fake fur; glue to face.

CAP

Since "a gnome without a cap is not a gnome," it is best to make your gnome's cap at this time. Cut one cap from red or gray felt, using pattern in individual directions. Sew side seam from base to tip; turn right side out. Stuff upper portion of cap with fiberfill until firm, leaving room for head. Pin or stitch cap to head.

PAINTING ON FABRIC

MATERIALS: *See individual crafts*

Use medium-weight muslin for painting; do not pre-soak fabric. Trace or enlarge pattern as directed. Transfer outlines of design to muslin as follows: Place muslin right side up on work surface; place graphite paper face down over fabric. Center pattern over the graphite and muslin, pin, and trace around lines of design with a hard lead pencil or dry ball-point pen. Remove pattern and graphite paper. The slightly waxy property of graphite will contain the paint within the outlined area and prevent spread of color to other areas.

For primary colors, dip tip of brush into desired color acrylic paint, then add three or four brushfuls of water and mix. Paint will have the look and consistency of weak tea. Practice on scrap fabric to get desired shade, then fill in area you are painting. If you are painting more than one color at the same time, leave space between colors to prevent bleeding; when paint is dry, go back and fill in space.

To shade areas, dip tip of brush into undiluted paint and lightly drag bristles through and around already painted areas. This will cause darker color to blend in with lighter color, and will give your painting added dimension. Turn any mistakes to your own advantage—no one will ever know that a stray line shouldn't be there.

After all paint has dried, go over major design lines with a No. 1 rapidograph pen. Add accents, facial features, and details with pen and watch your painting come alive!

The
Crafts
of
Christmas

The Day Before Christmas

Christmas is a special time for our family, a time for sharing and enjoying the traditions that are part of our Finnish, Danish, Polish, and German heritage.

Preparations begin on the first day of December, when the children — Genevieve, 8; Rodney, 6; and Gabrielle, 3 — begin earning stars for their Christmas Star Chart (the stars are given for completing chores, or for being generally kind and helpful, and they are sent to Santa with the gift lists). On that day also, the children begin taking turns removing the small packages attached to our Advent Banner. Each package contains a charm, a sweet, or a message, and as they disappear, it is a reminder to us of just how few days are left until Christmas.

On the day before Christmas, we all rise early, for there are many tasks yet to be done. After breakfast, my husband, John, sets off with Rodney to cut a spruce tree from the woods on our land. They may be gone all day, for some years the "best" tree is not easily found....

Welcome Sign

Note: Before beginning, read General Directions for Woodworking on page 16 for additional materials and directions.

SKILL LEVEL: Intermediate. Some knowledge of woodworking useful.

MATERIALS: Mahogany, 13 x 10 x 1″ (with grain along 13″ length). Plywood with mahogany veneer on one side, 13 x 10 x ³⁄₁₆″. Drill with ⁵⁄₁₆″ bit. Four ⁵⁄₁₆″ screws. ½″ wire nails.

DIRECTIONS: Use pattern to transfer design to mahogany. With drill, make starting hole through wood inside shaded area, which will be cut out. Using jig or coping saw, cut around design, watching out for

weak spots like tip of cap and gnome's hand. Using ³⁄₈″ straight firmer chisel, make stopcuts on letters, and complete following directions on page 16.

Using chisel closest in shape to lines of drawing, make stopcuts about ³⁄₁₆″ deep along dot/dash lines. Take No. 5 straight gouge and cut down to stopcuts, starting about ½″ away from figure to make him stand out from background. Next make stopcuts about ⅛″ deep all over rest of design along pencil lines to round figure and give it dimension. Starting with parts of figure that would be closest to you in reality, such as belt buckle, nose, and beard, shape these areas, following arrows. Cut deeper for parts farthest away from you, such as point of cap, ear, hair, axe, and squirrel. Some parts will have to be re-

drawn as you cut deeper into the wood. After cutting is completed, sand edge of figure and frame inside and out until smooth.

Using oil colors mixed with trace of turpentine, paint figure and letters, following photograph for color. Let dry for several days. Coat wrong side of carving with thin layer of waterproof glue. Position carved piece on mahogany side of plywood, matching edges carefully. Weight down and allow to

dry thoroughly. When dry, nail a few ½" nails into back around edges.

From right side, drill hole in each corner at dots for screws. Varnish as directed on page 16.

ADAPTATIONS: Write another message instead of "Welcome." Before joining back to front, glue in a favorite print or photo behind the gnome.

Enlarge on 1" squares; see page 16 for directions

Gnome Crossing Sign

Note: Before beginning, read General Directions for Woodworking on page 16 for additional materials and directions.

SKILL LEVEL: Intermediate. Some knowledge of woodworking useful.

MATERIALS: Mahogany, 11 x 8 x 1" (with grain along 11" length). One 18 x ⅜" dowel. Drill with ⅜" bit.

DIRECTIONS: Using pattern, transfer front view to mahogany. With drill, make starting hole through wood inside shaded area, which will be cut out. Using jig or coping saw, cut around design and inside shaded area, watching out for weak spots like tip of cap and feet. Place pattern for back view on back of cut piece, lining up edges; using pattern, transfer design, inserting letters from front onto back following diagram. Using ⅜" straight firmer chisel, make stopcuts on letters and complete following directions on page 16.

Using chisel closest in shape to lines of drawing, make stopcuts about 3/16" deep along dot/dash line on front and back. Take No. 5 straight gouge and cut down to stopcuts, starting about ½" away from figure to make him stand out from background. Next make stopcuts about ⅛" deep all over rest of design along pencil lines on front and back to round figure and give it dimension. Starting with parts of figure that would be closest to you in reality, such as hands and face on front and shoes on back, begin to shape these areas following arrows. Cut deeper for parts farthest away from you. Some parts will have to be redrawn as you cut deeper into wood.

After cutting is completed, sand edge of sign until smooth. Using oil colors mixed with trace of turpentine, paint figure

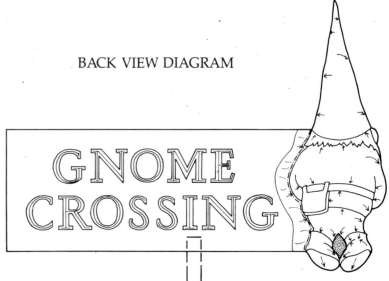

BACK VIEW DIAGRAM

and letters following photograph for color. Let dry for several days. Drill ⅜"-deep hole in base of sign, indicated on pattern by dash lines. Whittle one end of dowel to point; insert other end (and dab of glue) into

drilled hole. Varnish as directed on page 16.

ADAPTATION: Eliminate dowel and hang using eye bolts. Change the message to one of your choice.

GNOME CROSSING

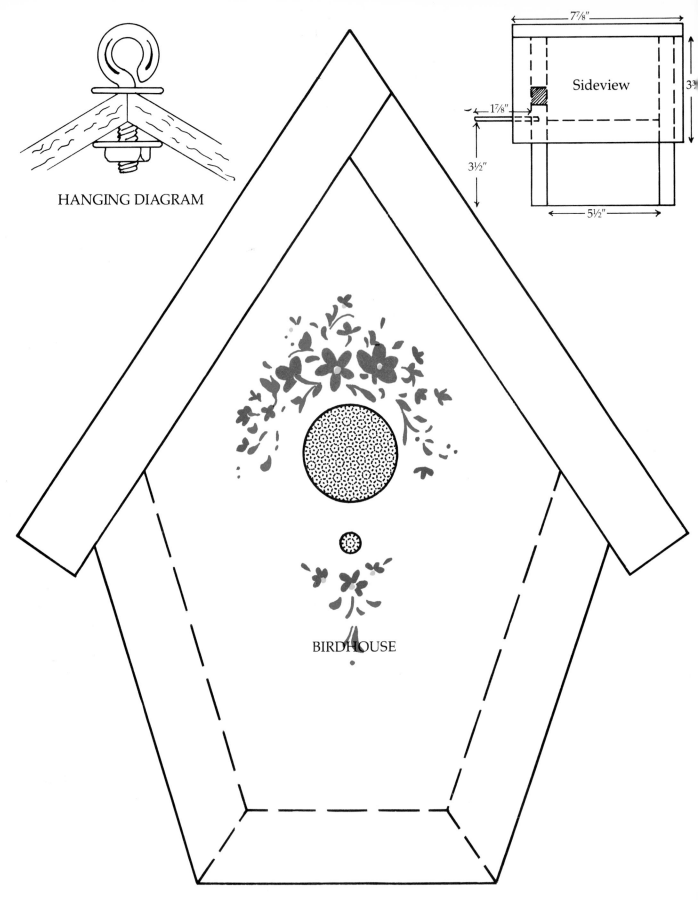

HANGING DIAGRAM

7⅞"

Sideview

3

1⅞"

3½"

5½"

BIRDHOUSE

CHART			
Bird	Diameter of Entrance	Height of Entrance Above Floor	Height of House Above Ground
Chickadee	1⅛"	6–8"	6–10'
House Wren	1–1¼"	1–6"	6–10'
Nuthatch	1¼"	6–8"	12–20'
Titmouse	1¼"	6–8"	6–15'

Birdhouse

Note: Before beginning, read General Directions for Woodworking on page 16 for additional materials and directions.

SKILL LEVEL: Intermediate

MATERIALS: Sharp pencil. Cork-backed steel ruler. T-square. One 5′ piece 1 x 8″ white pine. ¼″ dowel, 2¼″ long. Coarse, medium, fine sandpaper. Miter box. Waterproof wood glue. Drill with ¼″ bit. Copper or aluminum nails. Brass flathead screw. Two round brass pivot screws. Two eye bolts. Four washers. Two nuts. Waterproof all-weather paint, desired colors (*see Directions*). Medium and fine paintbrushes.

DIRECTIONS: With some general knowledge of the birds found in your area, decide upon the type of bird you wish to attract. With minor adjustments, this house will probably attract a chickadee, house wren, nuthatch, or titmouse. However, build the house for a specific bird; do not overlook the variations required for each species (*see Chart*). You can utilize this design to attract other types of birds if you alter the dimensions of the house; research the specifications in one of the many books available on birdwatching or birdhouses.

Use the same size pattern (or altered pattern) to mark two pieces on pine for front and back. Also mark 6⅛ x 7⅞″ left roof, 5⅜ x 7⅞″ right roof, two 5½ x 3½″ sides, and a 5½ x 3½″ bottom, using sharp pencil, cork-backed steel ruler, and T-square. Cut out using jig or coping saw. Using miter box, angle long edges of bottom, then angle upper and lower edges of sides following pattern. Sand cut edges *only*, with coarse, then medium, then fine sandpaper. Test pieces for fit as you go along, sanding edges as necessary to produce accurate, perfectly fitted joints.

Drill ventilation holes ½″ below top edges of side pieces; these will be covered by the roof extensions to prevent rain from entering during a storm. Drill ¼″ drainage holes in bottom, centering one along each side edge. Glue roofs together as shown, making sure the joint is tight. Nail joint to secure, using only aluminum or copper nails to prevent rusting. Following *Hanging Diagram*, drill ¼″ hole through peak of roof, about 2″ away from each end. Insert eye bolt with washer attached through hole, then attach washer and nut on inside. This will prevent water from leaking into house.

Following *Chart* for size, cut out hole in front piece for desired bird. Drill ⅜″-deep hole below opening for perch; glue dowel into hole. Glue house sides between front and back pieces; glue roof in place. Nail to secure. Position house over bottom piece. Attach bottom to sides at rear of house using brass pivot screws. Screw front of house to bottom using brass flathead screw. This will facilitate easy cleaning of interior of house after it has been inhabited.

Sand exterior of house, smoothing corners and joints. Do not paint, stain, or varnish interior, perch, or edge of entrance hole. Paint house as shown in photograph, or paint it in dull colors, which are more apt to attract birds. If desired, paint the design above the hole, following full-color pattern.

Hang birdhouse out in the open, where it will receive both light and shade. Do not position it in thick foliage, which may conceal enemies.

Gnome on a Swing

Note: Before beginning, read General Directions for Woodworking on page 16 for additional materials and directions.

SKILL LEVEL: Intermediate

MATERIALS: Mahogany, 20½ x 12 x 1″ (if you have a longer name than will fit comfortably on this width, start with a wider piece to allow for the extra let-

ters; the swing seat should be extended accordingly to balance the design). Clear pine, 1¼ x 12 x ¾″, for swing seat. Two 18 x ⅜″ dowels. Two ¾″ screw eyes. ⅜″ drill. Four 1¼″ wire nails.

DIRECTIONS: Using patterns, transfer front view and two extra hands and feet to mahogany. Using jig or coping saw, cut around design, including extra hands and feet (set these aside); sand. Place pattern for back view on back of cut piece, lining up edges; transfer. Trace name you wish to carve from alphabet on *Foldout A*; center and transfer it to tree bar, back and front. Using ⅜″ firmer chisel, make stop cuts on letters, back and front, following *General Directions for Woodworking*, page 16.

Using chisel closest in shape to drawing, make stopcuts

about ⅛″ deep along all pencil lines, except for hair lines, which will be incised lightly after all carving is completed. Cut deeply along dot/dash lines. Round wood following arrows, using appropriate gouges; omit carving hands and feet. Make deep cuts for parts of figure that would be farthest away from you, such as ears, and arms between hands and beard. Using No. 7 ⅜″ gouge,

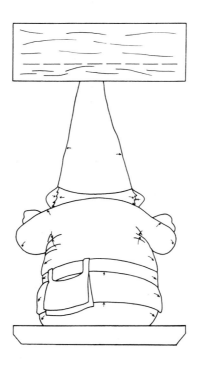

cut channel just deep enough to take thickness of dowel along dash lines on hands and extra hand pieces (*see Hand Diagram*). Position dowels through hands and mark where they meet tree bar; using ⅜″ drill, make two holes, each ½″ deep, in underside of tree bar, making sure to center hole in underside of wood to prevent splitting or running off the edge. Apply dab of waterproof glue to top end of each dowel and bang into place. Glue appropriate hand piece in place over hand and dowel; cramp in place to dry. When thoroughly dry, carve whole hand around dowel, and carve rest of sleeve. Apply glue to back of extra feet and cramp in place to main carving, lining up edges; let dry thoroughly. Round bottom of each sole, carving an instep along dash

line. Lightly incise hair lines on beard and head.

Following *Swing Seat Diagram*, cut away shaded areas of clear pine along fine dash lines. Position pine piece below carving, wide side up, centering wood so it protrudes in back and front of figure. Mark where dowels meet seat; drill holes all the way through wood in marked positions. Holding seat in place, mark where feet touch

HAND DIAGRAM

SWING SEAT

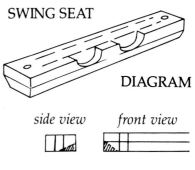

DIAGRAM

side view   *front view*

See Foldout A for sign pattern and alphabet

it. Lay feet over marks and mark where they cross seat. Following both of these marks, cut out U-shaped pieces using chisel and gouge. Position seat under figure to determine if fit is right; adjust as necessary; sand smooth.

Using oil colors mixed with a trace of turpentine, paint figure and letters, following photograph for color. After several days, apply dab of glue inside drilled holes and along base of figure. Press seat to figure, inserting dowels in holes. When dry, trim off ends of dowels, which are protruding through holes. If piece is a bit twisted, hold it correctly and nail through base of seat. Varnish as directed on page 16.

Drill two small holes equidistant from top ends of tree bar; insert screw eyes for hanging.

Meanwhile, the girls and I start the last
of the baking. In fact, we have been baking
all month — Finnish coffee bread (pulla)
and Danish pastries and a wonderful
gingerbread farmhouse where gnomes have
been known to hide. This day has been
saved for molding the marzipan figures
who inhabit the farmhouse, and for baking
cookies for Santa and for the carolers who
will come this evening. There is a Scandina-
vian tradition that all carolers are invited
inside for something to eat on Christmas Eve...

Gingham Aprons

SKILL LEVEL: Intermediate

MATERIALS: *For Each:* Prequilted gingham fabric, 45" wide.* White cotton fabric for lining, same yardage as for gingham. Extra-wide double-fold bias seam tape, grosgrain ribbon, 1" wide, both to match or contrast with quilted fabric.* Thread: white, red, navy, chartreuse, hunter green. Graphite paper. *For Females' Aprons:* Scrap red cotton fabric. Matching or contrasting ruffled shirred trim or ruffled eyelet trim, 1½" wide.* *For Males' Aprons:* Velcro fastening strip. Red six-strand embroidery floss.
**See Yardage Chart for yardage amounts.*

DIRECTIONS: *Females' Aprons:* Read General Directions for Appliqué on page 17. Enlarge and trace desired size patterns as directed. Use apron pattern to cut two pieces each from gingham and lining. Use pocket pattern to cut one piece from gingham. Transfer appliqué/embroidery design to right side of pocket. Use heart pattern to cut heart(s) from red fabric, adding ¼" seam allowance around edges. Machine-appliqué heart(s) in place. Using close zigzag satin stitch, machine-embroider design lines with navy thread. Sandwich all raw edges of pocket with seam tape as directed on tape package, and sew pocket to front of apron in position indicated on pattern.

Sew apron fronts to backs at shoulders, making one gingham apron and one lining. With raw edges even, sew ruffled eyelet trim around outer edges of gingham apron; overlap and finish ends. Cut ribbon in half; with raw edges even, sew one to each side of gingham front in positions indicated on pattern by slash marks. Pin gingham and lining together, right sides facing, with trim and ribbons sandwiched in between. Sew ¼"

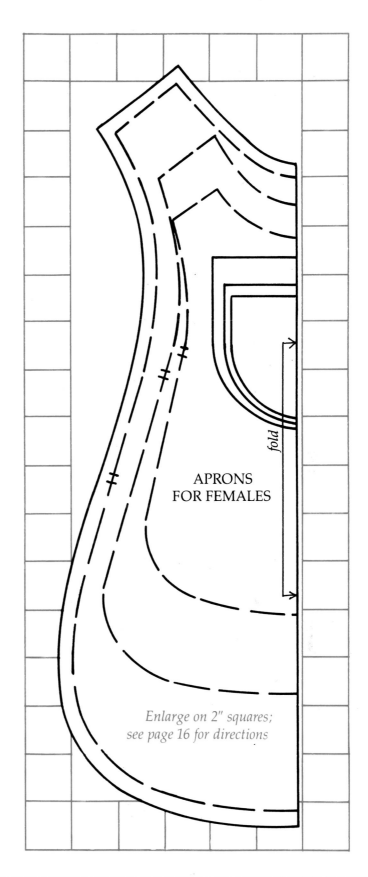

APRONS
FOR FEMALES

*Enlarge on 2" squares;
see page 16 for directions*

fold

YARDAGE CHART				
	Fabric	Bias Seam Tape	Grosgrain Ribbon	Trim
FEMALE:				
Child	½	2½	2	2¾
Girl	¾	2½	2½	3¼
Adult	1	3	3	4
MALE:				
Boy	½	2	2½	—
Adult	1	5½	3⅓	—

from raw edges, leaving neck open for turning. Turn to right side and press. Zigzag-stitch over seam of apron and trim so trim stands out. Baste neck edges of lining and apron together, matching shoulder seams. Starting at back, sandwich raw neck edges with bias tape, same as for pocket, and sew, overlapping ends of tape.

Males' Aprons: Enlarge and trace desired size patterns as directed. Use apron pattern to cut one piece from gingham and lining. Use pocket pattern to cut one piece from gingham. Transfer embroidery design to right side of pocket. Machine-embroider chartreuse and hunter green grass on pocket using a random straight stitch for grass (*see page 18*). Hand-embroider red gnome caps in grass. Sandwich top edge of pocket only with tape; turn bottom and side edges ¼" to wrong side; sew pocket to apron in position indicated on pattern. Pin lining to gingham with wrong sides facing. Sandwich raw edges of apron with bias seam tape, same as for pocket. Cut ribbon to fit around neck comfortably; roll and hem raw edges, then sew ends securely at top edges of apron where marked. Cut remaining ribbon in half; sew to sides of apron where marked.

For potholder on adult apron, cut a 10" square from gingham. Sandwich raw edges with bias

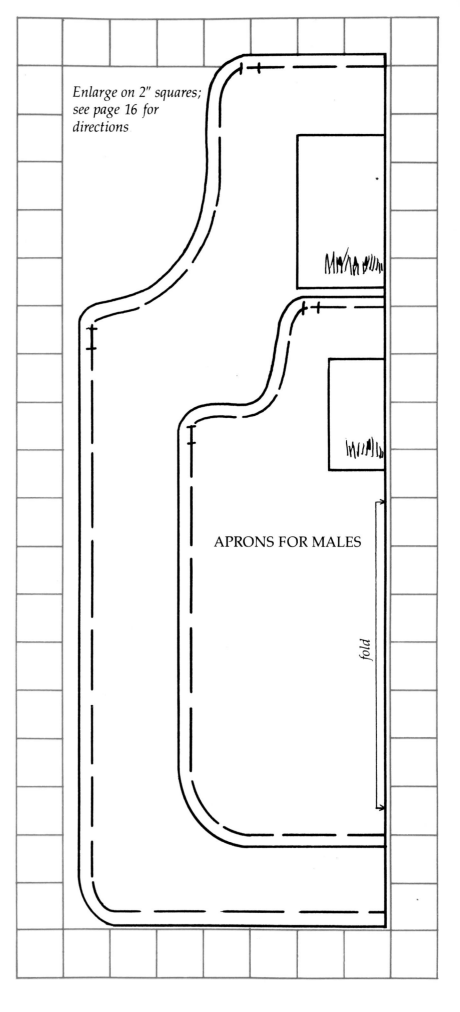

Enlarge on 2" squares; see page 16 for directions

APRONS FOR MALES

fold

tape, same as for apron; machine-embroider grass motif in one corner, same as for pocket.

Sew Velcro to wrong side of potholder and to right side of apron in desired positions.

ADULT FEMALE
POCKET MOTIF

CHILD'S POCKET MOTIF

GIRL'S POCKET MOTIF

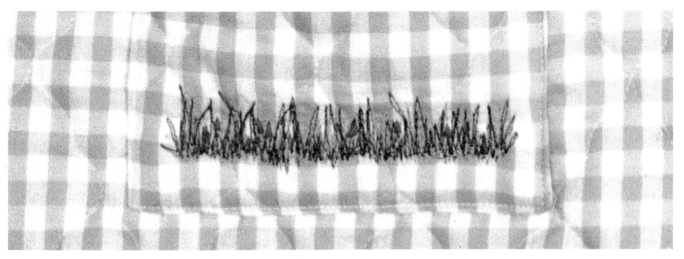

Cookie Bags

SKILL LEVEL: Elementary to Intermediate

MATERIALS: *For Drawstring Bag:* String. Pencil. Thumbtack. Tailor's chalk. Red cotton fabric, 45" wide, 1¼ yards each: gingham, polka dot. White ½" rickrack, 2½ yards. White cord, 1 yard. Thread. Sturdy cardboard. Paper for pattern. Spray adhesive. *For Gnome Tote:* Calico, 36" wide, ¼ yard each of two different prints. ½" rickrack, or other trim, ½ yard. Cord, ⅝ yard. Fusible nylon webbing.

DIRECTIONS: *Drawstring Bag:* Make compass using thumbtack, pencil, and 14" length of string. Tack one end of string to center of 29" square sheet of paper; tack pencil to other end. Swing pencil around to mark 28"-diameter circle. Following *Diagram A,* scallop edges of circle, adjusting scallops evenly. Using scalloped pattern, cut one piece each from gingham and polka dot fabric. Baste rickrack ½" away from scalloped edge of gingham piece on right side. With right sides facing, sew fabrics together, matching scallops and leaving opening

for turning. Clip curves and points. Turn to right side; slip-stitch opening closed; press. Draw a 20"-diameter circle in center of polka dot side of scalloped piece using tailor's chalk instead of pencil. Make casing by sewing two parallel lines ⅜" apart following marked circle. Slit polka dot fabric crosswise in one spot between lines of casing. Finish off raw edges of slit using button hole stitch (*see Embroidery Stitch Details, page 18*). Run cord through casing using safety pin; knot cord ends.

Cut a 10"-diameter circle from cardboard; a 12"-diameter circle

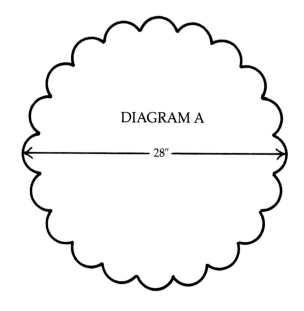

DIAGRAM A

28"

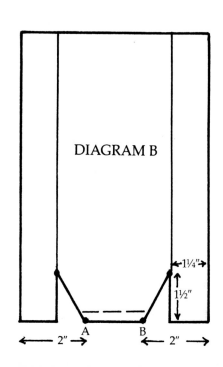

DIAGRAM B

1¼"

1½"

A   B

2"   2"

from gingham; and a 9"-diameter circle from polka dot fabric. Spray one side of cardboard with adhesive; center and smooth gingham over cardboard. Wrap edges to other side; glue in place. Glue polka dot circle over raw edges of gingham. Insert covered cardboard into bag; pull drawstring and tie, gathering top of bag.

Gnome Tote: Cut two 7½ x 9½" pieces from each calico; cut two 7½ x 9¼" pieces from fusible webbing. Press one 7½" edge of each calico piece ¼" to wrong side. Prepare fabric for exterior of bag as follows: Mark a point along pressed edge of two calico pieces, 4½" away from each side on both. Cut cord in half; pin ends at marked points on each piece, so cord forms a loop above fabric. Pin rickrack to wrong side along pressed edges (over cord), so rickrack extends above edge.

Place calico with rickrack wrong side up on work surface; center fusible webbing over fabric. Position other calico piece right side up over webbing, matching pressed edges to pressed edges. Press, fusing fabrics completely together and securing rickrack and cord. Topstitch.

With exterior sides facing, sew sides together along 9½" edges. Following *Diagram B,* measure 1¼" away from each side edge and 1½" up from bottom and mark spot with a dot. Clip through both front and back from bottom edge to dot. Measure in 2" from each side along bottom and mark with another dot. Clip from new dot to original dot on each side, and remove a wedge-shaped piece of fabric. Continuing to follow *Diagram B,* sew from point A to point B. Turn bag to right side. Using tailor's chalk, draw parallel lines 1¼" away from both side edges. Press along these lines and topstitch to hold folds. Tuck in flaps at bottom and tack to hold in place.

ADAPTATION: Use bags to hold items other than cookies.

Painted or Papered Gnome Cookies

SKILL LEVEL: Elementary

MATERIALS: Darning needle (optional). Fine and medium paintbrushes. Toothpicks. Small plastic bag.

RECIPES

DOUGH
1 cup butter or margarine
1 cup sugar
2 eggs
1 tsp. vanilla
3 cups unsifted all-purpose flour
1½ tsp. double-acting baking powder
½ tsp. salt

1. Combine softened butter or margarine and sugar and beat until creamy.
2. Add eggs and vanilla, beating well.
3. Add flour, baking powder, and salt and beat until well mixed.
4. Form two balls and chill for three hours.

ICING
2 egg whites
¾ tsp. cream of tartar
2½ cups confectioner's sugar
Food coloring: red, blue, green, yellow

1. Beat egg whites with whisk or electric beater until frothy and slightly thickened.
2. Add cream of tartar and continue beating until whites hold a peak.
3. Sift confectioner's sugar into whites, ½ cup at a time, beating thoroughly between adds.
4. Beat 5–8 minutes until icing is thick and smooth.
5. Set aside portion that will remain white (to be used for papered cookies and/or white sections on painted gnomes). Tint small portions of decorative icing in several small bowls by combining with food coloring until desired color is achieved. Make green, red, pink, yellow, blue, brown, and light brown icing.
6. Keep damp cloth over each bowl to prevent drying.

red

pink

white

blue

yellow

brown

pink

pink

blue

brown

light brown

DIRECTIONS: *Painted Cookies*
1. Trace patterns for male and female gnomes.
2. Roll out ball of dough to ⅛" thick.
3. Place gnome patterns on dough and trace around edges with knife or darning needle; remove pattern. Place cookies on sheets.
4. Bake at 350° F. for 8–10 minutes or until golden brown.
5. Cool on rack.
6. Using medium paintbrush, spread surface of cooled cookies with white decorative icing that has been thinned with 2 tsp. water.
7. Use toothpick to define design in areas to be painted.
8. Paint these areas with appropriate colors of tinted icing following pattern.
9. For facial features, combine orange and green undiluted food coloring to make brown. Using fine paintbrush, draw in features.

42

DIRECTIONS: *Papered Cookies*
1. Roll out ball of dough to ⅛" thick.
2. Cut out pictures of your choice from Christmas cards, or from prints on page 153. Place pictures on top of dough and trace ¼" away from edge with sharp knife or darning needle.
3. Remove prints and place cookies on cookie sheets.
4. Bake at 350° F. for 8–10 minutes or until golden brown.
5. Cool on rack.
6. Return picture to corresponding baked cookie shape; adhere to cookie with icing.
7. Fill small plastic bag with white icing and snip small hole in one corner. Squeeze icing out, covering edge of print.
8. Allow icing to set.

ADAPTATIONS: For a different effect, use tinted icing for outline, or combine a number of small pictures or photographs on one cookie.

43

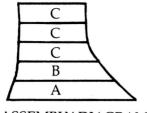

ASSEMBLY DIAGRAM

See Foldout B for full-size pattern for cutting cakes

Bûche de Gnome

SKILL LEVEL: Intermediate

MATERIALS: Cardboard, 12 x 14". Small plastic bags. Powdered chocolate. Confectioner's sugar. Natural greens.

RECIPES

CHOCOLATE CAKE
Use your favorite recipe and triple to make three 8 x 1½" layers and two 9 x 1½" layers.

CHOCOLATE ICING
Triple your favorite recipe.

DECORATIVE ICING
See Icing Recipe for Painted or Papered Gnome Cookies, page 41. Green food coloring only.

MERINGUE
3 egg whites

¼ tsp. cream of tartar
¾ cup granulated sugar

With mixer set at high speed, whip ingredients together until stiff.

DIRECTIONS: *Trunk*
1. Trace patterns for A, B, and C. Position patterns over cooled cakes and carefully cut around them with sharp knife, cutting one A, one B, and three C pieces.
2. Stack cakes on 12 x 14" cardboard following *Assembly Diagram*, icing in between layers with chocolate icing as you stack them.
3. Cut roots from excess cake; attach to trunk at bottom with chocolate icing.
4. Continue to ice entire trunk except for top surface.
5. Cut gnome picture for doorway from page 153. Back with aluminum foil to prevent grease

from spotting print, and position on trunk as shown in photograph.

6. Add extra icing for overhang on door as shown in photograph, and twist lumps of icing to form knots on roots.

7. For top, lighten chocolate icing with white decorative icing and apply, swirling knife over top to give surface added texture. To create jagged bark, pull knife upward on trunk sides until icing extends beyond lip of top layer.

DIRECTIONS: *Mushrooms and Petals*

1. Fill small plastic bag with meringue; snip a small hole in one corner. For mushroom caps, squeeze ten mound shapes onto brown paper. For ten stems, squeeze out meringue while slowly lifting bag. For petals, squeeze six teardrop shapes onto paper.

2. Bake meringue shapes in a slow oven (225° F.) for about 45 minutes, or until dry but not browned.

3. Remove from brown paper while still warm and cool.

4. To assemble mushrooms, scrape small hole in center of flat side of each cap to accommodate stem. Dip stem into white decorative icing; push stem gently into hole on underside of cap. Decorative icing will dry, securing cap and stem together.

5. Arrange mushrooms around trunk as shown in photograph.

6. Push petals into side of trunk over roots. Chocolate icing will hold in place.

7. Tint some white decorative icing with green food coloring. Using a plastic bag with a small hole in one corner, squeeze icing into leaf shapes at bases of petals.

8. Sprinkle mushroom tops with powdered chocolate. Arrange greens around bottom of trunk. Sprinkle confectioner's sugar liberally over entire trunk and greens to resemble snow. Arrange marzipan gnomes around trunk if desired.

Marzipan Gnome Family

SKILL LEVEL: Elementary

MATERIALS: *Marzipan*
1 lb. pure almond paste
1½ cups sifted confectioner's sugar
3 tbsp. light corn syrup
¾ tsp. vanilla
Also: Food coloring: red, blue, green, yellow. Paintbrush.

Mix first four ingredients together and knead until smooth. Following actual-size diagrams, shape gnomes by breaking off pieces of marzipan and rolling, flattening, or kneading them into desired shapes. For adult male gnome, roll ball for head; pinch top into point for cap. Make barrel shape for body, adding two rolls for legs and two flattened balls for feet. Make two rolls for arms. Attach all pieces with light pressure before marzipan hardens, smoothing seams. Shape parcel separately and place under hand area. Use knife to incise lines for clothes, hands, face, and beard.

For adult female, roll ball for head. Add flattened triangle for kerchief and secure under chin, trimming shape with knife. Pinch another piece of marzipan into pointed cap and add to head, smoothing seams. Connect barrel-shaped torso to bell-shaped skirt and attach to head. Make two rolls for arms and attach. Shape parcel separately and place under hand area. Use knife to incise lines for clothes, hands, and face.

For children, make smaller versions of male and female. Paint all gnomes with food coloring as desired.

ADAPTATIONS: Use family as ornaments. Use marzipan to sculpt animal shapes.

MARZIPAN FAMILY

Gingerbread Farmhouse

SKILL LEVEL: Advanced

MATERIALS: Darning needle (optional). Cardboard. Small plastic bags. Fine paintbrush. Natural greens. Powdered chocolate. Food coloring: red, yellow, green. Light yellow construction paper or cellophane.

RECIPES

GINGERBREAD
6 cups sifted all-purpose flour
4 tsp. ground ginger
1½ tsp. ground cinnamon
1 tsp. ground cloves
¼ tsp. each ground nutmeg, cardamom, salt
2 sticks butter or margarine
1 cup firmly packed light brown sugar
½ cup dark corn syrup
½ cup light molasses

1. Sift flour and all spices together in bowl.
2. Combine butter, brown sugar, corn syrup, and molasses in saucepan over low heat until butter is melted and all ingredients are blended. Remove from heat.
3. Add 2 cups flour mixture to butter mixture and blend well.
4. Continue adding remaining flour mixture, blending until dough is firm but pliable.
5. Flour hands and knead dough until smooth and slightly sticky. If dough is too moist, add flour by the tablespoon.
6. Refrigerate for one hour.

DECORATIVE ICING
See Icing Recipe for Painted and Papered Gnome Cookies, page 41. Triple recipe. Make icing while gingerbread bakes. Cover with damp towel to prevent drying. Icing will be used for decoration and assembly.

While dough is refrigerating:
1. Enlarge and trace patterns as indicated. Use to cut out cardboard templates for farmhouse. Cut an 8 x 11" piece cardboard to serve as base.
2. Coat two or three cookie sheets

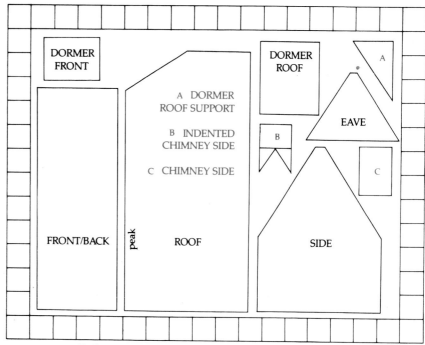

Enlarge on 1" squares; see page 16 for directions

with butter; sprinkle with flour and tap off excess.

3. Preheat oven to 325° F.

DIRECTIONS: *Making Farmhouse Sections*

1. Roll out dough to ¼" thick between sheets of waxed paper.

2. Using cardboard templates, cut around each section with sharp knife or darning needle; cut two roof pieces, two front/back pieces, two sides, one eave, one dormer roof, two dormer roof supports, one dormer front, two chimney sides, two indented chimney sides, two doors, about 1 x 2", and two stoops, 1 x ½". Cut 28 roof pieces, ¾ x ¼".

3. Place dough on cookie sheets and bake for 35 minutes or until cake is firm and brown. Bake roof pieces slightly longer if dark brown color is desired.

4. Cool all sections completely.

DIRECTIONS: *Decorating Farmhouse Sections*

1. Position all cooked gingerbread sections on work surface covered with wax paper; position four main sections so bottom edges are even as follows: side-front-side-back.

2. Apply white decorative icing evenly with flat knife or spatula, covering each piece completely.

3. Apply four small squares of white decorative icing to door pieces to resemble window panes, following photograph. Position doors on front and side or back as desired. Cut window print from page 153 and position as desired on front of house.

4. To make decorative beams for house exterior, tint some white icing with chocolate powder. Fill small plastic bag with the mixture; snip small hole in one corner of bag. Squeeze icing in a steady motion across all pieces in a straight line, making sure beams on end pieces will match when pieces are assembled; to prevent lumps, start stream of icing flowing before touching gingerbread. Enclose window and doors between beams, fol-

lowing photograph.

6. Paint "bricks" with undiluted red food coloring; add glow to door panes with undiluted yellow food coloring, separating individual panes with undiluted brown food coloring. Darken beams with undiluted brown food coloring.

DIRECTIONS: *Assembling Farmhouse*

1. Assemble farmhouse on 8 x 11" piece cardboard.

2. Cement sides with icing to front and back, then cement roof pieces in place so back edges are flush, and front edges protrude. Add eave, matching slashes.

3. Cement dormer supports and dormer front to one side of roof; attach dormer roof. Cut light yellow construction paper to size of dormer window and attach with decorative icing. Paint panes with brown food coloring.

4. Cement indented chimney sides over peak of roof; close off chimney with remaining chimney sides.

5. Decorate roof with white "snow" icing, following photograph.

6. Add fourteen roof pieces to each side of roof peak.

7. Add stoops in front of doors with blobs of white icing.

8. For soot in chimney, use freshly ground black pepper.

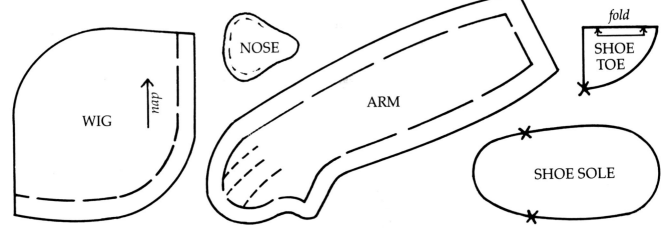

Kitchen Witch

Note: Before beginning, read General Directions for Soft Sculpture Head on page 18 .

SKILL LEVEL: Advanced

MATERIALS: Cotton fabric, 45" wide, ¼ yard each: muslin; brown/white calico; white/ brown calico; scrap white. Fiberfill. Acrylic paint: white, red, yellow, blue, steel gray, burnt sienna, orange. Brown felt-tipped fine line marking pen. Gray fake fur with at least a 2" nap. Scraps felt: red, green, brown, yellow. One child's ribbed sock. Branch, about ⅜" in diameter and about one foot long, or a ¼" dowel. Straw or straw-colored raffia. Two black seed beads. Matching thread. Sturdy cardboard. Glue. Pearl cotton for hanging.

DIRECTIONS: Cut 8"-diameter circle from muslin for head. Trace all patterns. Use patterns to cut out nose from muslin and two wig halves from gray fake fur. Complete head following directions on page 18.

Cut 6½ x 4" body from muslin. Use patterns to cut four arms and two legs from muslin. Fold body in half, matching 6½" edges; sew across long edge and one short edge, making a pouch. Turn to right side; baste around top edge. Stuff pouch with fiberfill until very firm. Insert head into opening and pull basting, enclosing fiberfill. Tie off. Push raw edges inside body, and slip-stitch head firmly to body. Sew a pair of arms and leg pieces, leaving open at tops; turn to right side. Stuff with fiberfill until firm. Fold raw edges inside and slip-stitch openings closed. Quilt hands along dash lines. Slip-stitch arms and legs to body.

Use pattern to cut two blouses from muslin. Sew cen-

48

ter front seam; press center back seams to wrong side. Sew side and underarm seams; hem edges of sleeves and bottom of blouse. Clip neck edge to seamline and press to wrong side. Baste around hem on each sleeve; place blouse on witch. Pull basting on sleeves, gathering fabric to fit wrists. Slip-stitch back edges of blouse together.

Cut a 26 x 7½" skirt from brown calico. Sew short edges together, making a circle of fabric; hem one edge 1", then baste around opposite edge. Place skirt on witch, pulling basting to gather top. Slip-stitch hemmed edge of blouse securely over raw edges of skirt.

For apron, cut 9 x 5" apron and 26 x 1½" tie from white calico. Hem one long and two short sides of apron; hem all edges of tie. Gather top of apron to 4¼" width; center on tie and fold tie in half, sandwiching raw edges of apron. Topstitch; tie around waist.

Use pattern to cut two socks from child's sock, positioning ribbing as shown on pattern; sew sides. Turn to right side and pull one onto each leg; fold down at marked line. For slippers, cut four soles from brown felt, two soles from cardboard, and two toe pieces from brown felt. Sandwich cardboard between felt soles; glue. Sew toe piece around end of each sole, matching X's. Slip-stitch slipper to each foot at toe.

Use pattern to cut four birds and four wings from white fabric. Make two flat bird halves and wings by sewing two pairs together, leaving an opening in each for turning. Turn to right side; stuff lightly with fiberfill and slip-stitch openings closed.

Machine-quilt along dash lines. Whip-stitch bird halves together around front between marked dots. Paint beak orange. Stuff head and open back of body with fiberfill. Sew wings to sides in marked positions. Cut two legs from yellow felt; sew to bottom of bird. Cut one cap each from red and green felt; whip-stitch sides and stuff each cap with fiberfill. Insert caps into back of bird and tack to stuffing inside bird.

To make broom, tie straw or raffia to one end of branch. Run branch under witch; attach bottom of body to branch so one leg is on each side. Wrap left hand around branch; tack. Wrap right arm around bird's neck; tack. Attach pearl cotton to back of witch's neck for hanging.

ADAPTATION: Use as a tooth-fairy. Dress in "fairy" colors.

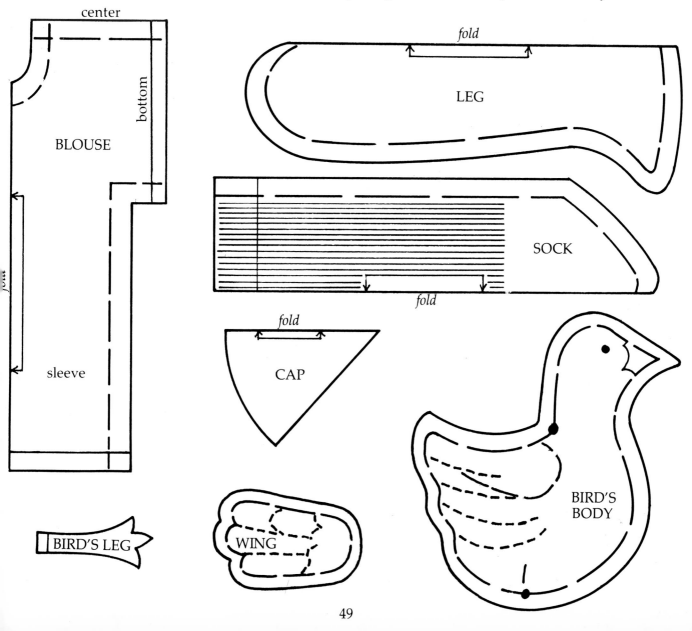

A few last-minute decorations will ready
the house. From the cedar chest come
the carved members of a twelve-piece
angel orchestra, which we place on a linen
cloth that my mother embroidered when
she was a girl. We get out the Christmas
quilt, and Grandma Tasa's china for the
smorgasbord supper. The girls hang red
hearts from every nook and cranny. And
at last the "men" are home, glowing with
the news that this year they have found
the "best" tree ever.

Appliquéd Pillows

Note: Before beginning, read General Directions for Appliqué on page 17.

SKILL LEVEL: Intermediate

SWINGING GNOME PILLOW

MATERIALS: Cotton fabric, 45" wide: muslin: ⅓ yard; kelly green polka dot, ½ yard; white/green calico, green gingham, ¼ yard each; green, ⅛ yard each: bright calico, dark calico, polka dot, solid. Cotton scraps: red, blue, yellow, brown. Scrap fake fur. Gold pearl cotton. Fiberfill. Thread to match fabrics. Paper for pattern. Graphite paper.

DIRECTIONS: Cut an 11¾" square background from muslin; transfer appliqué design to center using graphite paper. Using separate patterns for jacket, pants, and swing, cut pieces from blue, brown, and yellow fabrics respectively. Hand-appliqué all other pieces to background in marked positions following directions on page 17. Sew jacket to pants; fold raw edges under and hand-appliqué over marked lines on background, leaving small opening in pants bottom for stuffing. Stuff jacket and pants with fiberfill until plump. Stitch closed, easing pants as necessary. Fold swing in half with right sides facing and sew short sides; turn to right side and stuff with fiberfill. Fold raw edges inside and stitch below pants so swing protrudes from background. Knot pearl cotton; run up through swing seat at marked X's, through arms, and "wrap" around appliquéd branch as shown. Hand-appliqué cap in position, leaving bottom open. Stuff cap lightly with fiberfill. Glue scrap of fake fur for hair under cap. Stitch cap closed.

Cut 24 patchwork pieces,

each 2¾" square, from various green fabrics. Machine-sew two groups of five and two groups of seven squares together, pressing seams open. Sew short strips to side edges of background with raw edges even, then sew long strips to top and bottom edges with raw edges even.

For ruffle, cut four 44 x 2¼" pieces each from white/green calico and green gingham. Sew short ends of matching strips together, making two large circles of fabric. Sew circles together along one edge with right sides facing; turn to right side and press. Sew two rows of machine basting close to raw edges; gather ruffle to fit pillow front, and sew in place, easing ruffle around corners. Cut a 16¼" square backing from green polka dot fabric; sew to pillow front with right sides facing, leaving an opening for turning. Turn to right side and stuff with fiberfill. Fold raw edges ¼" inside, then slip-stitch opening closed.

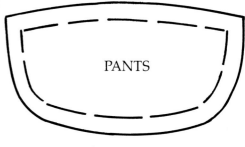

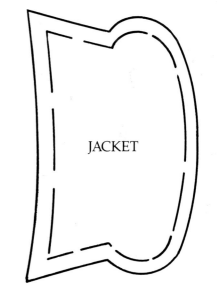

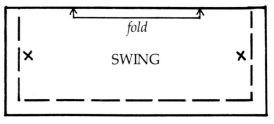

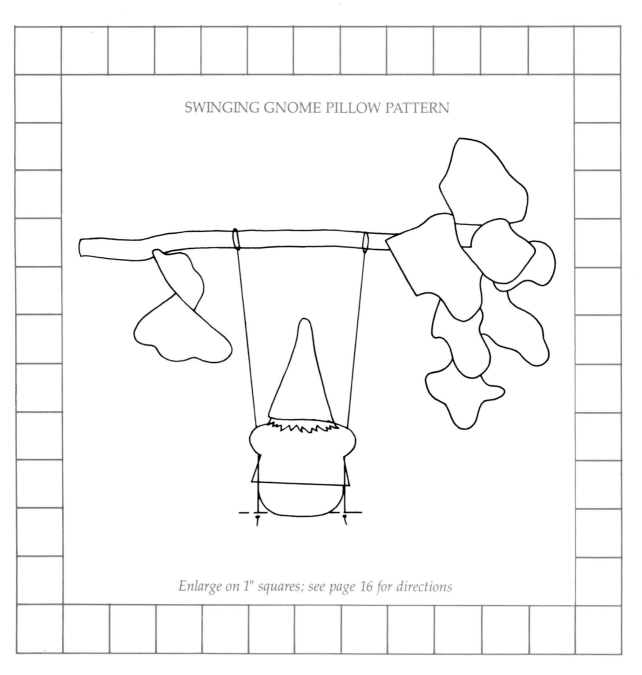

SWINGING GNOME PILLOW PATTERN

Enlarge on 1" squares; see page 16 for directions

GNOME WITH HEART PILLOW

MATERIALS: Cotton fabric, 45" wide: white, ⅝ yard; blue, ⅛ yard each: solid, polka dot, gingham, calico. Scraps cotton: red, pink, green, red polka dot. Six-strand embroidery floss: black, white, red, pink, brown. Green grosgrain ribbon, ¼" wide, 6". Novelty piping, 2⅜ yards blue polka dot. Thread to match fabrics. Fiberfill. Graphite paper.

DIRECTIONS: Cut a 16½" square background from white fabric; transfer appliqué design to one corner at an angle using graphite paper. Using pattern, cut two pieces for red heart from polka dot fabric; sew together with right sides facing, leaving opening for turning. Turn to right side, stuff with fiberfill, and slip-stitch opening closed; tack to background in marked position. Using patterns, cut appliqué pieces for cap, face, hands, beard, shirt, and tree, following photograph for colors. Hand-appliqué all pieces to background in marked positions following directions on page 17; stuff beard lightly with fiberfill before stitching closed.

Using six strands of brown embroidery floss in needle, satin-stitch tree trunk; using three strands, satin-stitch black eyes, white eyebrows, and red mouth; using three strands pink, outline-stitch around nose and lower eyelids; using three strands brown, outline-stitch string for heart (*see Embroidery Stitch Details, page 18*). Tie green ribbon into bow and tack above heart.

Cut 36 patchwork pieces, each 2½" square, from various blue fabrics. Sew two groups of eight and two groups of ten together, pressing seams open. Sew short strips to side edges of background with raw edges even, then sew long strips to top and bottom edges with raw edges even. Sew piping all around pillow front with raw edges even, easing around corners. Cut a 20½" square backing from white fabric; sew to pillow front with right sides facing, leaving an opening for turning. Turn to right side and stuff with fiberfill. Fold raw edges ¼" inside, then stitch opening closed.

HEART

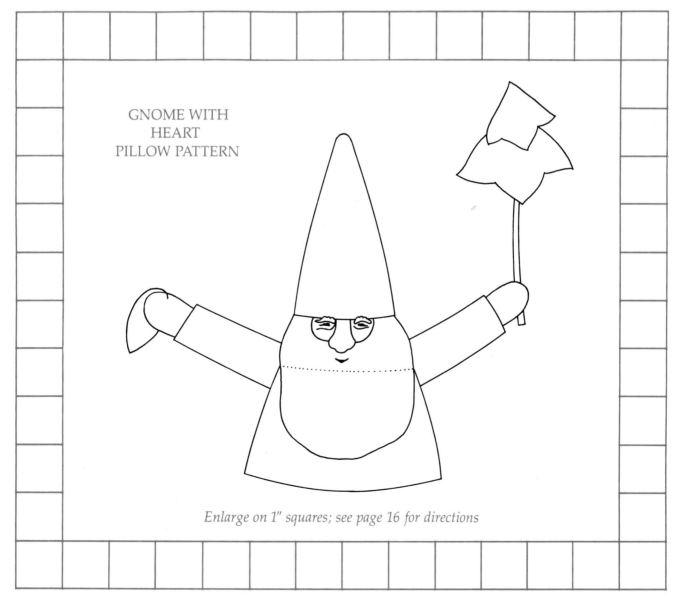

GNOME WITH
HEART
PILLOW PATTERN

Enlarge on 1" squares; see page 16 for directions

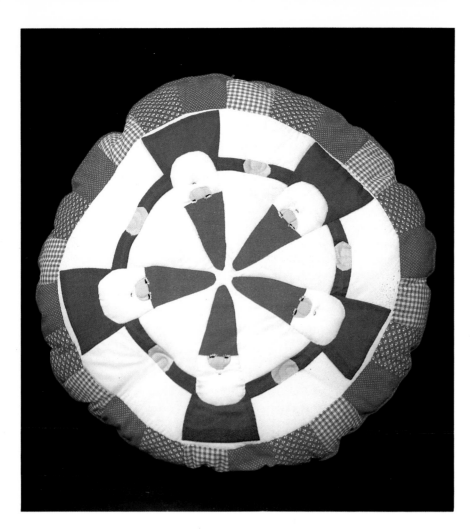

GNOMES IN A CIRCLE PILLOW

MATERIALS: Cotton fabric, 45" wide: white, 1½ yards; blue, ¼ yard; red, ⅛ yard each: solid, polka dot, calico, gingham; scrap pink. Six-strand embroidery floss: white, black, red. Novelty piping, 2½ yards red polka dot. Thread to match fabrics. Fiberfill. String. Pencil. Thumbtack. Graphite paper.

DIRECTIONS: Make compass using thumbtack, pencil, and 13" length of string. Tack one end of string to center of 27" square sheet of paper; tack other end to pencil. Swing pencil around to mark 26"-diameter circle. Use circle as pattern to cut two pieces from white fabric; set aside one piece for backing.

Mark exact center of background pillow piece. Use appliqué pattern to mark five gnomes radiating outward from

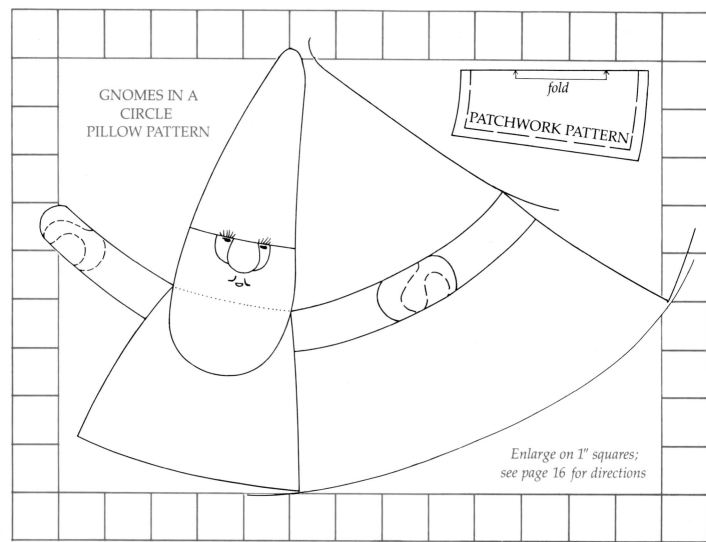

GNOMES IN A
CIRCLE
PILLOW PATTERN

fold

PATCHWORK PATTERN

*Enlarge on 1" squares;
see page 16 for directions*

center; the tips of their caps should each be about ½" away from center. Link hands as shown in pattern by incomplete adjacent gnome. Using patterns, cut appliqué pieces for cap, face, hands, beard, and shirt from fabrics following photograph, and hand-appliqué all pieces to background in marked positions following directions on page 17. Stuff beards lightly with fiberfill before sewing closed. Using three strands of embroidery floss in needle, outline-stitch black eyes, red mouth, and white moustache; straight-stitch white eyebrows (see *Embroidery Stitch Details, page 18*). Use pink thread to quilt hands in curving pattern as shown.

Use patchwork pattern to cut 24 patchwork pieces from various red fabrics. Sew together, making large circle of patchwork; press seams open, then press inner edge of circle ¼" to wrong side. Hand-appliqué to background around inner edges. Sew red piping all around pillow front with raw edges even, then sew front to back with right sides facing, leaving an opening for turning. Turn to right side and stuff with fiberfill. Fold raw edges ¼" inside, then slip-stitch opening closed.

Wildflower Frame

Note: Before beginning, read General Directions for Painting on Fabric on page 20.

SKILL LEVEL: Intermediate

MATERIALS: Cotton fabric, 45" wide, ⅓ yard each: muslin; red polka dot. Red polka dot piping, 2 yards. Red grosgrain ribbon, ¼" wide, 4". Matching thread. Graphite paper. Acrylic paint: colors listed in *Color Key*. Fine paintbrush. Rouge. Rapidograph pen. Sturdy cardboard. Batting. Spray adhesive. White glue. Thumbtacks. Decorative paper.

DIRECTIONS: Trace pattern and use to mark two frame outlines on muslin; cut out along cutting lines for inner and outer edges. Transfer design to muslin that will be front of frame using graphite paper. Paint design following *Color Key*. Lightly blend in red-orange on cheeks, nose, and tip of ear. Paint flower centers dark blue; paint petals lighter blue. Go over all lines of design and add details with rapidograph pen. Sew piping to front side of painted frame along inner and outer edges with raw edges even; to end piping, cut ½" of cord out of one end, turn edges of empty fabric tube to inside, and insert other end into opening.

For backing, draw line centered between inner and outer edges of remaining muslin piece following *Diagram A.* Cut backing into two pieces along line to make facings. With right sides together and piping in between, sew facings to edges of painted frame. Turn to right side and press lightly.

Using pattern minus seam al-lowance, cut out two cardboard frames; cut out interior section on one piece only. Cut batting to fit this piece and glue to one side. Position painted muslin over batting; wrap facings to cardboard side evenly so piping is centered over side edges and fabric is stretched evenly. Glue facings to cardboard, holding in place with tacks until glue dries.

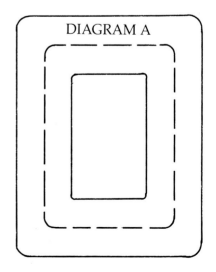

DIAGRAM A

Cut decorative paper to fit wrong side of frame border; glue in place, covering raw edges of facings.

For frame back, center remaining piece of cardboard on red polka dot fabric; cut fabric 1½" bigger than cardboard all around. Spray one side of cardboard with adhesive; center and smooth fabric over cardboard. Wrap raw edges evenly to other side and glue in place. Cut out a 9½ x 11½" piece of decorative paper, rounding corners; glue over raw edges of red fabric.

Cut a 9 x 2½" stand from cardboard; cut a 10 x 5½" piece from red polka dot fabric. Fold fabric in half lengthwise; sew long edge and one short edge together, making sack; turn to right side. Insert cardboard into sack; sew sack closed next to end of cardboard. Fold raw edges of ¾" excess fabric ¼" to inside and topstitch in place. Measure 9" above bottom edge of frame back on polka dot side; mark 2½" line parallel to bottom edge and centered between sides at this spot. Position excess fabric end of stand over this line, with stand facing top; slip-stitch stand securely to back along marked line. Fold stand down. Attach ribbon to stand and back 2" below stitched edge of stand. Glue papered side of back to papered side of padded frame around sides and top. Insert picture through bottom.

COLOR KEY
A White
B Flesh
  (see page 19)
C Red-orange
D Yellow
F Blue
G Lime green
H Grass green
J Brown
K Gray
L Plum

FRAME

FELT PIECES

Padded Books

SKILL LEVEL: Advanced

GNOME ACTIVITY BOOK

MATERIALS: Cotton fabric, 45" wide, ⅓ yard each: blue polka dot; white. Scrap red polka dot fabric. Clear plastic, 18" square, .008 thick. Red grosgrain ribbon, ⅜" wide, 1 yard. White, blue flannel, one 6½ x 9½" piece each. Assortment of felt squares in many colors. Thread to match fabrics. Batting. Sturdy, medium-weight cardboard, two 6 x 9" pieces and two 5½ x 8½" pieces. Decorative paper.

DIRECTIONS: For outer cover, cut 23 x 9½" piece from blue polka dot fabric; place right side up on flat surface with long edges at top and bottom. Trace pattern and use to cut one heart from red polka dot fabric; pin heart to lower right corner of cover piece, spaced 2" in from side and bottom edges. Machine-appliqué heart in place following directions on page 17. Make a 2¼" hem along opposite side (9½") edge, then fold hemmed edge down 6" to right side of fabric for pocket; press. Cut batting to fit folded fabric; baste batting to wrong side of fabric without attaching it to

pocket. Baste pocket in place at top and bottom.

For inner lining, cut a 6 x 9½" left lining and an 8½ x 9½" right lining from white cotton. Cut a 10 x 9½" underpocket, and a 5 x 9½" overpocket from plastic; fold each in half, matching 9½" edges. Following *Gnome Activity Book Diagram*, place folded underpocket on left lining piece with raw edges even at top, bottom, and right side. Baste together along raw edges; sew pocket to lining across center as shown by fine solid line. Insert gnome print, cut from page 153, between folded edges of overpocket; sew along each side of

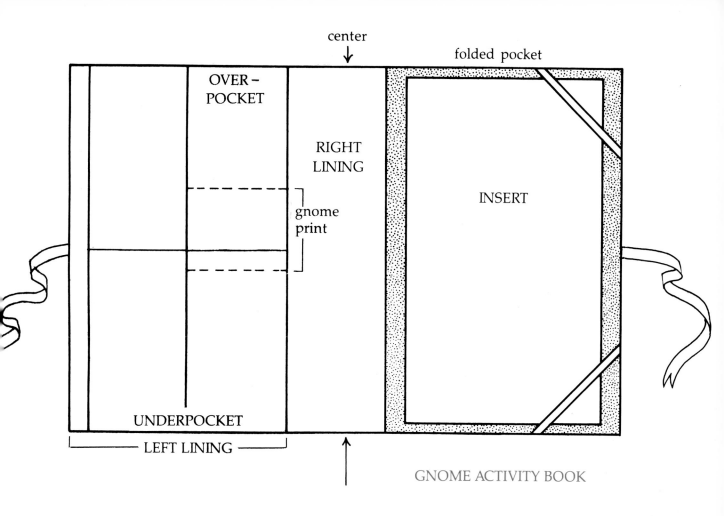

center

folded pocket

OVER‑POCKET

RIGHT LINING

gnome print

INSERT

UNDERPOCKET

LEFT LINING

GNOME ACTIVITY BOOK

HEART APPLIQUÉ

print to secure, following fine dash lines on diagram. Position overpocket on top of under‑pocket with raw edges even; baste together. Pin right lining to left lining along 9½" edges with plastic in between and raw edges even; sew, then open flat. Make a ¼" hem along right side edge of right lining. Cut 12" length of red grosgrain ribbon; with raw edges even, sew to center of left side edge of lining.

With right sides facing and raw edges even, pin lining to outer cover so plastic pockets are on same side as appliquéd heart. Sew together along top, bottom, and unfolded side; turn

61

to right side. Insert two 6 x 9" pieces of cardboard through opening, pushing one to each side of book; remove basting holding batting in place. Cut two 4" lengths of ribbon; turn raw edges ¼" to wrong side on an angle (*see Gnome Activity Book Diagram*) and sew. Attach ends of ribbons to corners as shown. Cut 12" length of ribbon; sew end of ribbon to center of right side. Cover end with a red felt heart.

For flannel boards, center flannel over remaining pieces of cardboard; fold raw edges ½" to wrong side all around and glue in place. Cut a piece of decorative paper and glue over raw edges of flannel. Place one flannel board into cloth pocket; place the other over same pocket, slipping two corners under the red ribbons. Cut a number of 5 x 2¾" pieces from the various colors of felt; store in sections of underpocket. Using patterns, cut out a number of male and female gnomes, houses, and trees from felt. Store in overpockets, along with a small pair of scissors. Felt pieces will stick to flannel boards and can be arranged to form many different designs.

GNOME SCHOOL SUPPLIES BOOK

MATERIALS: Cotton fabric, 45" wide, ⅓ yard each: red polka dot, red gingham. Scrap white/red calico. Red grosgrain ribbon, ⅜" wide, 1 yard. Clear plastic, 15" square, .008 thick. Velcro fastening strip, 6" long. Batting. Thread to match fabrics. Sturdy, medium-weight cardboard, two 6 x 9" pieces. Notepad, 5 x 7". Child's picture, 1½ x 2".

DIRECTIONS: For outer cover cut 14 x 9½" piece from red polka dot fabric; place right side up on flat surface with long edges at top and bottom. Trace letter patterns on page 124, and use to cut out child's initials from white/red calico; pin to lower right corner of cover piece as desired. Machine-appliqué initials in place following directions on page 17. Cut batting to fit cover and baste to wrong side of fabric.

For inner lining, cut one 10 x 9½" left piece and one 8 x 9½" right piece from red gingham. Fold 9½" edge of left piece 2" to wrong side and press. With right side of fabrics facing up, and with top and bottom (9½") edges even, overlap pressed edge 2" over right piece; topstitch together 1" away from and parallel to pressed edge.

Cut 4 x 9½" piece plastic and ¾ x 9½" strip of red polka dot fabric. Fold plastic in half, matching 9½" edges; position on right side of gingham as in *School Supplies Book Diagram* and baste along raw edges. Press one long edge of dotted strip ¼" to wrong side; with raw edges even, pin to gingham over plastic; topstitch close to pressed edge, securing plastic.

Cut the following from plastic for left side of inner lining: one 4¼ x 2¼" flap, one 8½ x 2½" change pocket, and one 13½ x 4¾" lower pocket. Cut 1½"-wide strips red polka dot: two 4¾" lengths and one 2½" length, for binding flap and change pocket edges, and one 7¼" length for

FELT PIECES

62

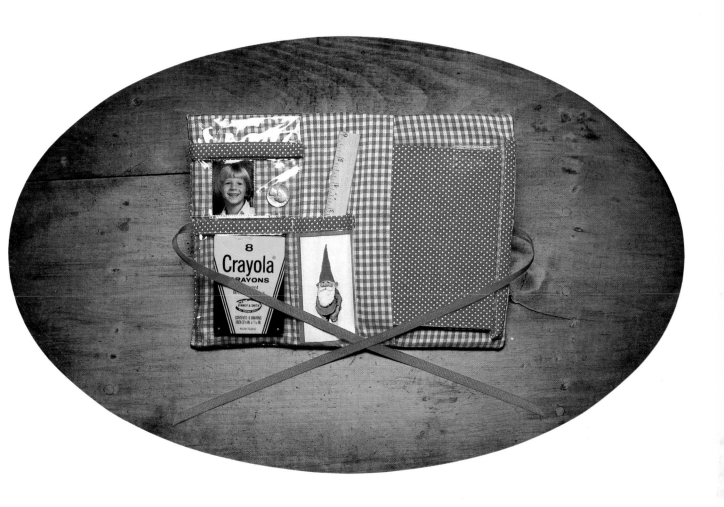

GNOME SCHOOL SUPPLIES BOOK

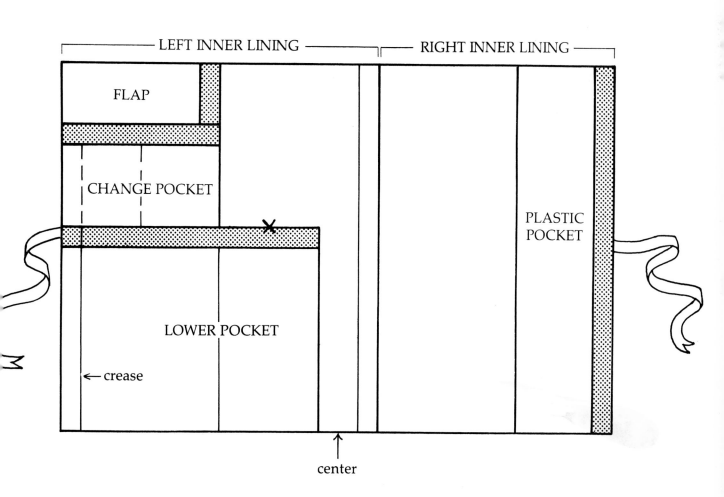

binding lower pocket. Press all long edges ¼″ to wrong side, then press bindings in half lengthwise, matching pressed edges.

For side of flap, sandwich right raw edge of plastic with 2½″ binding, leaving ¼″ extended on top; topstitch to plastic. For bottom edge of flap, sandwich raw edge with 4¾″ binding, leaving ¼″ extended on left and right sides. Topstitch to plastic. Fold ¼″ on right side under flap and tack. Sew piece of Velcro in L-shape at corner on wrong side of flap. With raw edges even, baste flap into top lefthand corner as shown in *School Supplies Book Diagram.* Sew one piece of Velcro to lining so it matches the Velcro on *side* of flap.

For change pocket, fold plastic in half with fold at right, matching 2½″ edges. Insert child's picture between layers of plastic and sew along each side to secure (shown as fine dash lines on *Diagram*). Sandwich upper edge of pocket with 4¾″ binding, leaving ¼″ extended on left and right sides. Topstitch to plastic. Fold ¼″ on right side under pocket and tack. Sew piece of Velcro to binding at right corner of pocket. Sew change pocket to lining so binding on flap covers binding on pocket.

For lower pocket, fold plastic in half, matching 4¾″ edges; sandwich top edge with 7¼″ binding, leaving ¼″ extended on left and right sides. Topstitch to plastic. Fold ¼″ on right side under pocket and tack. Make a ¼″ pleat 1″ away from left side edge of pocket; crease plastic with fingers, slip-stitch binding at top to secure. Sew lower pocket to lining; tack binding to lining at X; stitch print of your choice into lower pocket.

Cut red ribbon in half; with raw edges even, stitch ends to right side of lining, centered between top and bottom on each side. Sew lining to outer cover with right sides facing and raw edges even, leaving 6″ opening at bottom for turning. Turn to right side. Insert cardboard pieces into left and right halves of book. Fold raw edges at opening ¼″ to inside and slip-stitch closed. Remove basting.

Cut 5 x 7″ piece from red polka dot fabric. Using spray adhesive, glue red polka dot fabric to front cover of notepad; insert pad into plastic on right side of book.

STATIONERY CARRIER

MATERIALS: Cotton fabric, 45″ wide, ⅓ yard each: green/white plissé; muslin. Green grosgrain ribbon, ⅜″ wide, 3 yards. Ruffle eyelet trim, 1″ wide, 2 yards. Thread to match fabrics. Batting. Acrylic paint: white, red, blue, green, yellow, pink. Tailor's chalk. Dry ball-point pen.

Rapidograph pen. White charcoal paper for pad. Sturdy, medium-weight cardboard, two 6 x 9″ pieces for carrier backing; additional for pad. Waxed dental floss. Stationery in neutral color, 5 x 3½″ size. White glue.

DIRECTIONS: For outer cover, cut 14½ x 9½″ piece from plissé fabric. Trace pattern and use to cut circle from muslin; transfer design to fabric using graphite paper and dry ball-point pen; trace an initial in center of circle. Paint flowers, varying colors, with white centers; paint green leaves and initial. Following *General Directions for Appliqué* on page 17, hand-appliqué circle to right side of plissé, centered between top and bottom, and 2¼″

CIRCLE APPLIQUÉ

$$\mathcal{A}\,\mathcal{B}\,\mathcal{C}\,\mathcal{D}\,\mathcal{E}\,\mathcal{F}\,\mathcal{G}\,\mathcal{H}\,\mathcal{I}$$
$$\mathcal{J}\,\mathcal{K}\,\mathcal{L}\,\mathcal{M}\,\mathcal{N}\,\mathcal{O}\,\mathcal{P}\,\mathcal{Q}\,\mathcal{R}$$
$$\mathcal{S}\,\mathcal{T}\,\mathcal{U}\,\mathcal{V}\,\mathcal{W}\,\mathcal{X}\,\mathcal{Y}\,\mathcal{Z}$$

ALPHABET FOR STATIONERY CARRIER

center

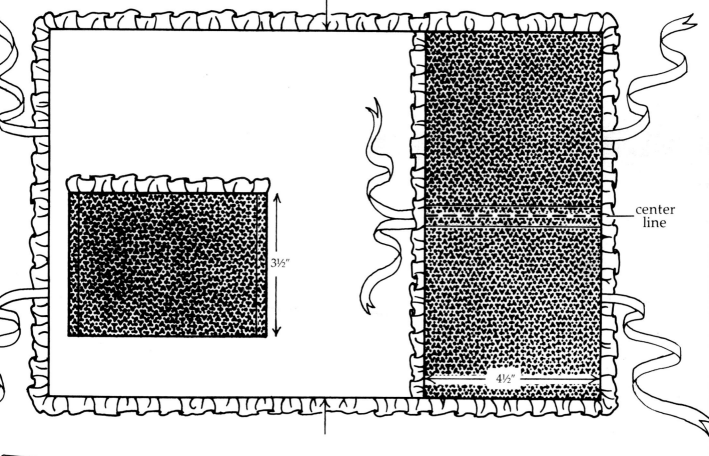

center line

3½"

4½"

Cut

CORNER FOLD
DIAGRAM

STATIONERY CARRIER

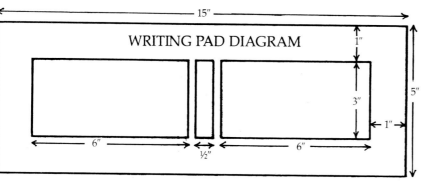

WRITING PAD DIAGRAM

15"

1"

3"

5"

1"

6"

½"

6"

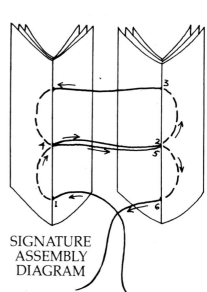

SIGNATURE
ASSEMBLY
DIAGRAM

away from right side (9½") edge. With right sides facing and raw edges even, sew ruffled eyelet trim all around outer cover; sew ends of eyelet together. Cut four 16" lengths of grosgrain ribbon; sew two to each side edge, 2½" away from top and bottom (*see Stationery Carrier Diagram*). Cut batting to fit cover and baste to wrong side.

For inner linings, cut 14½ x 9½" carrier lining, 12 x 5" large pocket lining, and 5½ x 4" small pocket lining from muslin. Cut 12 x 5" large pocket and 5½ x 4" small pocket from plissé; sew eyelet trim to one long edge of each pocket same as for outer cover. For large pocket, sew pocket liner to green pocket at long edge with right sides facing and raw edges even and eyelet trim in between. Turn to right side and press. Baste raw edges together. Using tailor's chalk, draw line on green side of pocket, dividing it in half crosswise; draw parallel lines 1½" away from center line on each side. Fold fabric along these lines, forming two pleats, and press with muslin sides facing; topstitch close to each fold. Pin large pocket to right side of lining with raw edges even at side edge (*see Stationery Carrier Diagram*), and with center line of pocket at center of side edge of lining. Sew pocket to lining along center line. Fold pleats so topstitched edges meet over center line; tack at top and bottom. Baste pocket to lining at top and bottom edges. Cut two 10" lengths of ribbon; attach one end to muslin beneath pocket and other end to pocket; tie ribbons into bow.

For small pocket, sew pocket liner to pocket around all sides with right sides facing and raw edges even and with eyelet trim in between at top, leaving opening for turning. Turn to right side; slip-stitch opening closed. Make ⅛" pleat ½" away from each side edge of pocket; topstitch in place. Slip-stitch pocket to left side of liner, ½" away from side, and 1½" above bottom.

Sew outer cover to lining with right sides facing and raw edges even, leaving 6" opening at bottom for turning. Turn to right side. Insert cardboard pieces. Fold raw edges at opening ¼" to inside and slip-stitch opening closed. Remove basting from batting. To decorate stationery, paint small motif in one corner of each piece. Insert stationery and envelopes into small pockets on right side.

To make writing pad, cut two 3 x 6" cover pieces and one 3 x ½" spine from sturdy cardboard. Cut 15 x 5" piece of muslin for cover. Following *Writing Pad Diagram,* center cardboard pieces on one side of muslin; mark positions lightly with pencil, then pick up each piece. Spray one side of each cardboard piece with adhesive, and glue pieces in marked positions. Fold raw edges over cardboard; glue in place, cutting corners at an angle to hide edges (*see Corner Fold Diagram, page 65*). Transfer and paint circle motif on front of pad, omitting initial.

Cut two 10" lengths of ribbon; center and glue ends at short sides of cover so ribbons extend outward. Cut two pieces of decorative paper 11¾ x 2¾" for endpapers. Glue half of each endpaper onto each cover, covering raw edges of muslin up to spine.

To make two signatures, cut ten 11½ x 2½" pieces of charcoal paper. Fold each in half crosswise; stack folded sheets in two groups of five sheets each. Machine-sew down fold lines. Using dental floss, stitch signatures together following *Signature Assembly Diagram* on page 65, pulling thread taut and knotting free ends together when finished. Run thin line of white glue along binding of signatures; insert signatures into spine of book and hold until glue dries. Glue endpapers to signatures along spine.

Advent Banner

Note: Before beginning, read General Directions for Painting on Fabric on page 20.

SKILL LEVEL: Elementary

FINISHED SIZE: Fits a 37 x 18" frame

MATERIALS: Muslin, 36" wide, ½ yard. Royal blue polka dot fabric, 45" wide, ½ yard. Embroidered yellow star patch. Graphite paper. Acrylic paint: colors listed in *Color Key.* Fine and medium paintbrushes. Rapidograph pen. Two snaps. 24 plastic 1" curtain rings. Batting. Matching thread. Sturdy cardboard, 37 x 18". Frame of your choice.

DIRECTIONS: Enlarge pattern on *Foldout A* as indicated. Draw a 32¾ x 13½" rectangle on muslin; transfer design to center of rectangle using graphite paper. Following *Color Key* and directions below, paint design. Numbers on pattern indicate very light (1), light (2), or dark (3)

shades of the same color; for letters with no number, paint section in a medium shade.

Paint sky first, gradually fading turquoise from deep shade at top to very light shade above trees. Paint trees on horizon with dark turquoise next, making treetops appear spiked; do not clearly define individual trees, but suggest distant shapes. For outlined trees closer to foreground, use turquoise color to accentuate some of the boughs and to suggest shadows beneath trees. A "ghostly" effect is achieved by brushing white paint over sections of trees, without covering trees entirely. Don't worry if some graphite lines are not covered; this enhances the ghostly effect.

Paint large tree next. Suggest spiked boughs in grass green sections first; mix turquoise and grass green paint on branches in sections where indicated. Suggest shadows at sides and bottom of tree with turquoise blending into light gray, then pale gray. Finally, paint snow (see photograph), filling in each section completely.

Paint all gnomes next. Paint faces and hands flesh; blend in pink for cheeks with touches of red. For each adult male gnome, paint white hair and beard, red cap highlighted with orange, blue shirt, light brown belt, yellow buckle, and gray boots. Paint young male gnomes, minus beard and belt, in same way; paint brown suspenders. For adult female gnomes, paint white hair, dark gray cap highlighted with medium gray, medium gray kerchief, light gray blouse with plum cuffs and trim, and grass green skirt shaded to simulate folds. Paint center adult female's torso following *Color Key*. Paint young female gnomes with yellow hair, lime green cap highlighted with grass green, white blouse, very light brown boots, and red cuffs and skirt shaded to simulate folds.

Paint remainder of design following *Color Key*. Paint fruit in shades of pink, orange, and red, highlighted with yellow. Highlight snow under gnomes' feet and simulate shadows with light blue. After all painting is

completed, outline and highlight all painted areas (except trees) with rapidograph pen.

Sew two male snaps to muslin at circled X's; sew female snap to wrong side of star. Attach star to muslin below bird until Christmas Day, when it moves to the top of the tree!

For border, cut two strips each 32¾ x 4¼", and two strips each 21 x 4¼" from blue polka dot fabric. With right sides facing, sew long strips to top and bottom edges of muslin; press seams open. Sew short strips to each side edge; press seams open. Attach 24 rings, evenly spaced around border, for hanging little gifts and trinkets of your choice.

For mounting, cut batting to fit cardboard and glue to cardboard. Center banner over batting, pulling excess fabric to back side while keeping design straight and even; tape raw edges to cardboard, then frame as desired.

See Foldout A for pattern

Needlepoint Fir

SKILL LEVEL: Intermediate

FINISHED SIZE: 10 x 13½″

MATERIALS: Double-mesh needlepoint canvas, 14-mesh-to-the-inch, 14 x 17½″. DMC Pearl Cotton #3, one skein of each color listed in *Color Key,* unless otherwise indicated in parentheses. Masking tape. Black waterproof felt-tipped fine line marking pen. Tapestry needle. Scissors. *For Blocking:* Brown paper. T- or carpenter's square. Rustproof thumbtacks. Softwood surface.

DIRECTIONS: Tape all raw edges of canvas with masking tape. Mark a 10 x 13½″ outline in center of canvas with waterproof marking pen, leaving 2″ margins around edges. You may want to stretch canvas on stretcher frame before beginning the work to avoid repeated blocking after completion of the piece; however, this makes the work bulky and difficult to carry around. Mark center guidelines on your canvas to facilitate blocking after the piece is finished: baste a line (using sewing thread) horizontally and then vertically across center of canvas, being careful to follow one row of mesh all the way across. Basting threads will cross in center.

One mesh of the canvas, formed by the intersection of horizontal and vertical threads, is represented by one square on the *Chart* (on double-mesh canvas, treat two adjacent threads as one). Each symbol on the *Chart* represents a colored stitch: follow *Color Key* to match colors with symbols. All squares without symbols (the background) are worked in pale blue.

Cut pearl cotton into 18″ lengths. Work design in Half-Cross Stitch, also known as the simple Tent Stitch. Start at upper left corner of section to be

worked. Work tree first, then work background to marked outlines. To start first strand, hold about 1″ of pearl cotton on back of canvas, and anchor it in place with the first few stitches. Cover first mesh as shown in stitch detail; insert needle in space below stitch just made, then repeat. Complete first row in this way; turn canvas around to work return row. To end a strand or begin a new one, weave end of pearl cotton under stitches on back of canvas. Try to keep tension of stitches firm and even. If pearl cotton twists while you are working, allow needle to hang straight down to untwist strand. If you make a mistake, pluck out yarn; do not reuse yarn.

Blocking: Mark exact size of canvas on brown paper using T-square; also mark horizontal and vertical guidelines. Place worked canvas face down over guide on softwood surface, matching center lines of guide to lines basted on canvas. Fasten to softwood surface using rustproof thumbtacks, spaced about ½″ apart all around perimeter of design; you may have to stretch canvas to match the guide. Wet canvas thoroughly with cold water and let dry. If necessary, block piece a second time in same way. Frame your needlepoint tree as desired.

See Foldout A for Chart

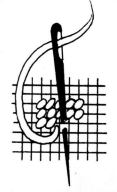

HALF-CROSS STITCH

Christmas Eve

After smorgasbord, John gets the tree from outside and sets it up in the living room. Our most cherished and abundant ornaments are the woven heart baskets, which the children fill with candy. My mother taught me how to cut and weave them from shiny, colored paper when I was a child. Now my children weave new ones from scraps of fabric cut from outgrown clothes. Many of our ornaments are selected for their memories... a wooden spool for thread that my Finnish grandmother saved for no reason; a paper chain Rodney made in nursery school; a swimming medal with a bright red ribbon that Genevieve won at a meet.

When the tree is finally decorated, John places the star on top and I place one package for each child on the tree skirt. After the children have hung their stockings they are allowed to open this gift. It is always the same each year — a pair of pajamas or a nightgown — but they get excited nonetheless.

Before we know it the carolers are at the door....

Forest Gnome Ornament

Note: Before beginning, read General Directions for Painting on Fabric on page 20.

SKILL LEVEL: Elementary

MATERIALS: Muslin, ⅓ yard. Graphite paper. Acrylic paint: white, blue, gray, gold, yellow, red, brown. Rapidograph pen. Thread. Fiberfill. Pearl cotton for hanging.

DIRECTIONS: Trace then transfer patterns for body front, back, and four legs (reverse pattern for two legs) to muslin using graphite paper. Paint muslin following photograph. Outline and highlight painted areas with rapidograph pen, paying special attention to details in face.

Let paint dry, then cut out entire figure. Sew front to back with right sides facing and raw edges even, leaving bottom open for turning; turn to right side. Baste around bottom edge of body. Stuff body with fiberfill until firm, pushing stuffing to tip of cap and ends of arms. Sew two pairs of legs together with right sides facing and raw edges even, leaving opening for turning; turn to right side and stuff legs until firm. Flatten tops of legs so seams and X's match. Insert into body, matching X's; pull basting, gathering body to fit around legs. Slip-stitch legs to body, pushing all raw edges of body inside. Draw bird tracks on soles, following detail. Tack hands together at back. Run 6″ length pearl cotton through peak of cap and knot ends together.

ADAPTATIONS: Use as doll for stocking stuffer. Glue to wood base for desktop companion.

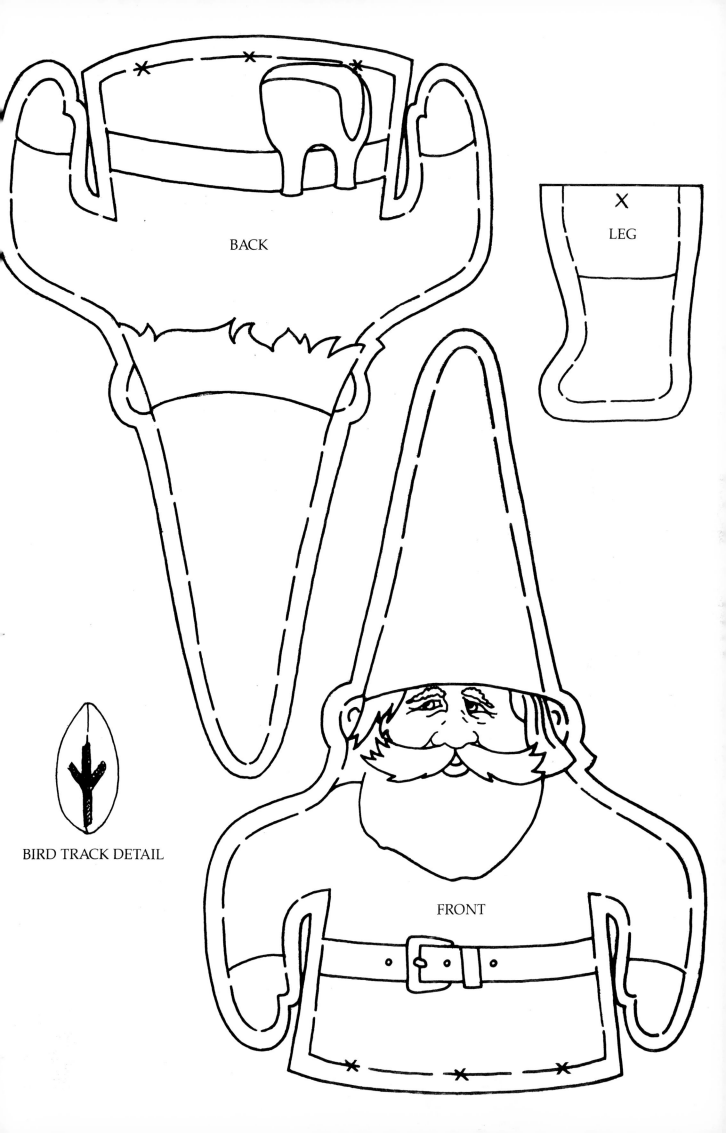

BACK

LEG

X

BIRD TRACK DETAIL

FRONT

Mouse in a Cap Ornament

SKILL LEVEL: Elementary

MATERIALS: Large scraps felt: red, gray, light green, dark green. Red, gray thread. Fiberfill. Red, black seed beads. Red pearl cotton.

DIRECTIONS: Trace patterns. Use to cut one cap from red felt; whip-stitch side edges together. Stuff peak of cap with fiberfill. Cut two body pieces from gray felt; whip-stitch together, leaving opening at bottom for stuffing. Stuff until very firm; whip-stitch opening closed. Roll up two 2 x 1″ strips of gray felt for arms; sew to each side of body at X. Attach two black seed bead eyes at large dots. Make tailor's tack whiskers with gray thread as indicated on pattern. Cut two ears and long strip for tail from gray felt; fold ears along dash lines and slip-stitch to head along placement line. Glue tail so it hangs from tip of cap. Insert mouse into cap; slip-stitch ends of arms over edge of cap as if mouse is grasping the edge. Cut three leaves each from light and dark green felt; glue at random inside cap behind mouse. Glue red seed beads to leaves for berries. Attach red pearl cotton for hanging.

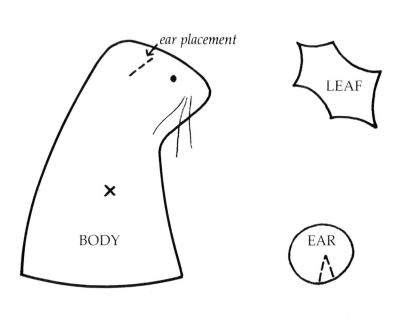

ear placement

LEAF

BODY

EAR

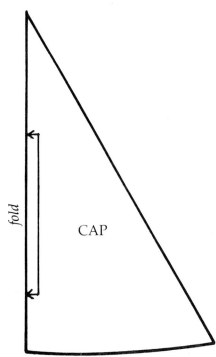

fold

CAP

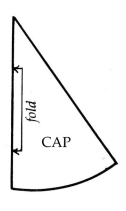

CAP

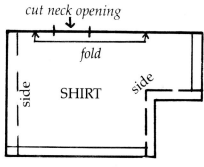

cut neck opening

fold

side   SHIRT   side

Gnomes in a Nest

SKILL LEVEL: Elementary

MATERIALS: Scraps felt: red, green. Red fabric for blanket, 3" square. Gold pearl cotton. Fiberfill. Rice grass or another dry grass. Bits of tissue and thread.

DIRECTIONS: Sew small bunches of rice grass together, forming a small nest as shown in diagram; insert bits of tissue and thread between the rice grass as you sew. Fill center of nest with fiberfill. Cut one small triangle each of red and green felt and roll up into tiny cone-shaped caps; whip-stitch sides of each to secure. Insert caps into nest, side by side. Cut small circle of red fabric; press raw edges to wrong side. Tuck blanket around fiberfill, covering bottoms of caps and all fiberfill. Secure pearl cotton to sides of nest for hanging.

Gnome in a Walnut

SKILL LEVEL: Elementary

MATERIALS: Walnut. Gold paint. Gold cord, 8" long. Scraps felt: red, gold, gray, flesh; muslin; blue cotton fabric. Fiberfill. Matching thread. Red, black, brown felt-tipped fine line marking pens.

DIRECTIONS: Open walnut, leaving at least one half of shell intact; eat nut. Paint intact half gold. Glue ends of cord inside shell for hanging.

Trace patterns and use to cut a red cap, two flesh hands, two gold pants legs, and two gray boots from felt; cut one shirt from blue fabric. Cut 2½"-diameter circle from muslin for head. Fill center of muslin with fiberfill and tie off. Sew side seams of shirt piece together; insert head into neck opening and slip-stitch in place. Hem sleeve and shirt bottoms. Stuff shirt lightly with fiberfill. Whip-stitch hand piece together and stuff lightly with fiberfill and insert inside sleeve; slip-

stitch. Whip-stitch side seams on each leg; gather bottom edge of each. Whip-stitch front and bottom seams on each boot. Stuff legs and boots with fiberfill. Insert bottom of each leg into boot; slip-stitch. Insert legs into bottom of shirt and tack in place. Glue fiberfill to head, forming hair and beard. Draw black eyes, brown nose, and red cheeks on face. Make cap by whip-stitching side edges together; stuff lightly with fiberfill, and glue over top of head.

Glue gnome into walnut shell; position arm so it rests on stomach, and tack in place.

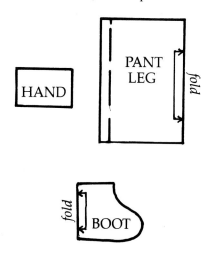

HAND

PANT LEG   fold

fold   BOOT

Woolly Sheep Ornament

SKILL LEVEL: Intermediate

MATERIALS: Large scrap white flannel. Heavy weight, natural color fisherman's wool. Felt scraps: white, black. Matching thread. Pearl cotton for hanging. Fiberfill. Acrylic paint: white, black, blue. Rouge.

DIRECTIONS: Cut 3¼ x 3½" rectangle from white flannel. Fold in half with right sides facing and raw edges even; sew long sides together. Turn to right side. Hand-baste around edge of one end; then pull basting tightly to close end, making pouch. Stuff pouch with fiberfill, then hand-baste around edge of opening, pulling basting tightly to close.

Trace face pattern and use to cut one face from black or white felt. Machine-sew dart in face. Baste along dash lines between marked X's, gathering gently to form shallow pouch. Stuff pouch lightly with fiberfill and slip-stitch face to one end of body. For woolly coat, make small, tight loop with wool; secure loop to rear end of body with stitch. Cover entire body surface with loops, working around body from rear to front in tight spirals (*see Coat Diagram*). Do not cut wool until last loop is made, then tack end of last loop down. Using patterns, cut four legs and two ears out of black or white felt. Roll each leg into a tube and whip-stitch to hold. Slip-stitch legs to underside of body. Glue ears in place in row of wool next to face. Paint white or black eyes in appropriate place on face. Dab blue on centers of eyes for pupils. Apply rouge if cheeks are white. To hang, thread a length of pearl cotton through wool loop on top of sheep and tie ends together.

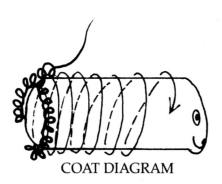

COAT DIAGRAM

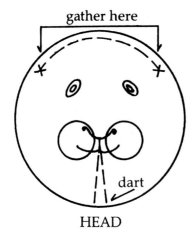

gather here

dart

HEAD

EAR

Little Gnome in a Snowball Ornament

SKILL LEVEL: Intermediate

MATERIALS: Oven-bake modeling compound. Acrylic paint: red, white, yellow, blue, brown, gray. Plastic foam ball, 3" diameter. Small kitchen knife or orange stick. Acrylic varnish. Pearl cotton for hanging. Needle. White glue.

DIRECTIONS: Fashion a gnome from modeling compound following actual-size *Sculpting Diagram* for front and side views. Use knife or orange stick to carve face, beard, and edges of cap, sleeves, and pants legs. Bake gnome for 15 minutes in a 325° F. oven, checking often to prevent scorching. Remove and cool. When cool, paint gnome with acrylics following photograph; when dry, apply one coat of varnish.

Cut plastic foam ball in half; scoop out 1½" wide x 1" deep hole from center of one half to accommodate gnome. Place gnome in hole and cut groove in perimeter to fit cap; this will be the top. Remove gnome. Run needle with knotted pearl cotton through foam from inside groove for cap through top of ball; make a loop for hanging at end. Glue gnome into snowball, covering knot.

To make a little standing gnome, see photograph for shape and follow directions for baking and painting.

ADAPTATIONS: Reduce size and use as pendant, light pull, or cake decoration.

SCULPTING DIAGRAM

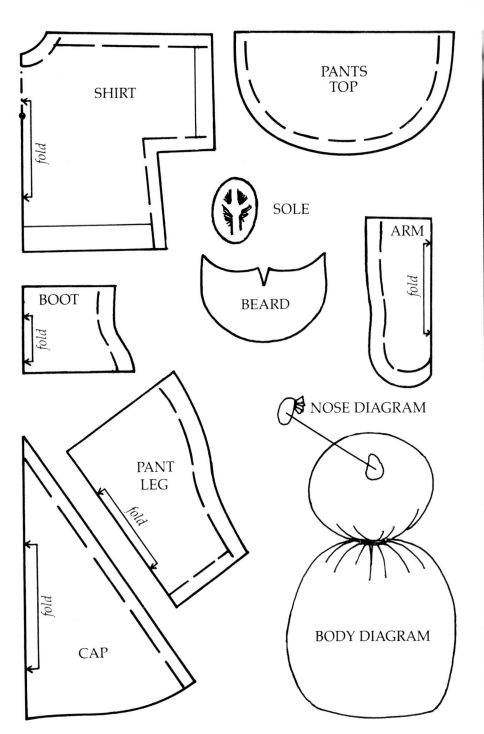

Gnome & Mushroom

SKILL LEVEL: Intermediate

MATERIALS: Large scraps cotton fabric: blue, red polka dot, muslin. Scraps felt: red, pink, brown, gray. White fake fur. Matching thread. Fiberfill. Flesh-tone nylon stocking. Red pearl cotton for hanging. Black felt-tipped fine line marking pen. Rouge.

DIRECTIONS: For nose, cut a 3"-diameter circle from single layer of nylon stocking. Push portion of fiberfill (size of ½ cotton ball) into nylon; compress by tying off close to fiberfill. Shape nose as in *Nose Diagram*. Trim excess nylon to ⅛" from tie (finished nose is about ¼" in diameter). For head, cut a 4"-diameter circle from stocking. Push portion of fiberfill (size of 4 cotton balls) into stocking. Finish as for nose (finished head size is about 1½" in diameter). Position nose in upper half of head (*see Body Diagram*) and slip-stitch to head.

Trace pattern and use to cut beard from white fake fur; glue beneath nose and trim neatly. Cut hair from narrow strip of fur and glue around back of head. Cut small bits of fur for eyebrows and moustache; glue in place. Draw in eyes with black marking pen. Rub rouge onto nose and cheeks. Trace pattern and use to cut cap from red felt; sew along seam, turn to right side, and tack to head.

For gnome's body, cut 3" square from stocking. Fold in half and sew one long and one short side, forming pouch. Turn to right side and stuff with fiberfill. Baste around opening; pull basting tight and tie off. Slip-stitch gathered end of body to head, hiding raw edges (*see Body Diagram*).

Trace pattern and use to cut two shirts from blue fabric; clip

stem to arm to secure. Slip-stitch other arm behind gnome's back. Attach pearl cotton to top of cap for hanging.

Mushroom Cluster Ornament

SKILL LEVEL: Elementary

MATERIALS: Large scrap muslin. Large scrap red polka dot cotton fabric. Green grosgrain ribbon, ¼″ wide, ¼ yard. White seed beads. Fiberfill. Compass. Red pearl cotton for hanging.

DIRECTIONS: For stems, cut three strips from muslin, each about 3 x 2½″; fold in half lengthwise. Sew along long edge and one short edge of each strip; turn to right side and stuff firmly with fiberfill. For caps, use compass to mark three 3″-diameter circles on red polka dot fabric. Cut out circles and press raw edges ¼″ to wrong side. Baste along pressed edges, then pull thread gently to gather circles into pouches. Stuff pouches with fiberfill; insert open ends of stems into caps and pull basting tight, gathering caps around stems; tie off basting. Slip-stitch caps to stems securely. Sew beads onto caps at random. Cluster mushrooms together and secure with green grosgrain ribbon tied in a bow. Attach red pearl cotton to top of one mushroom for hanging.

ADAPTATION: Use as a pin cushion.

one piece along dot/dash line for front. Sew shirt pieces together with right sides facing. Turn to right side; hem bottom and sleeves. Slip shirt over gnome. Trace pattern and use to cut two arms from pink felt. Sew seams on each arm; clip curves and turn inside out. Stuff arms lightly with fiberfill, then insert into sleeves with hands extending below sleeve hem; slip-stitch in place. Trace patterns and use to cut two pants legs and two pants tops from brown felt. Sew curved edges of trousers together. Clip curves and turn inside out. Slip over bottom of body and slip-stitch in place. Sew seams on each leg; turn inside out and stuff with fiberfill. Flatten legs slightly with seam at back. Slip-stitch top of each leg to trousers toward back of body (this gives gnome the look of having a pot belly). Trace patterns and use to cut two boots and two soles from gray felt; draw bird track on each sole with black marking pen. Sew front boot seams; turn inside out. Slip boots over bottom of each leg; glue sole to bottom of each boot and leg.

Make mushroom following directions for *Mushroom Cluster Ornament* at right. Wrap one arm around stem; slip-stitch

Woven Heart Ornament

SKILL LEVEL: Elementary

MATERIALS: Large scraps of two different calico fabrics, one light, one dark. Matching thread.

DIRECTIONS: Trace pattern and use to cut four heart tops each from light and dark calico fabrics. Press straight edges ¼" to wrong side. With right sides facing and raw edges even, sew matching-color pieces together around curved edges. Clip curves; turn to right side.

Cut four 1½ x 6" strips from each fabric. Fold each strip in half with right sides facing and long edges together. Sew ⅛" from long edge on each, making eight tubes; turn to right side and press with seam centered on one side. Each strip should be ⅝" wide. Cut a 1⅜ x 9" handle from one fabric; make same as for strips, pushing raw ends inside and slip-stitching closed.

With center seams facing up, insert ends of four strips ¼" into matching heart tops so strips are neatly capped at each end (*see Diagram A*); slip-stitch pressed straight edges of heart tops over strips. Fold strips in half, with seams inside, matching curved edges of heart tops. Press.

Position folded hearts on work surface as shown in *Diagram B*. Weave strips as shown in *Diagrams C* and *D*. When weaving is completed, straighten woven sections by pulling gently in both directions. Sew handle inside basket at inner points of heart as in *Diagram D*. Fill with candy and hang.

ADAPTATIONS: Make heart from decorative paper. Fill with dried flowers rather than candy. Use as favor on Valentine's Day.

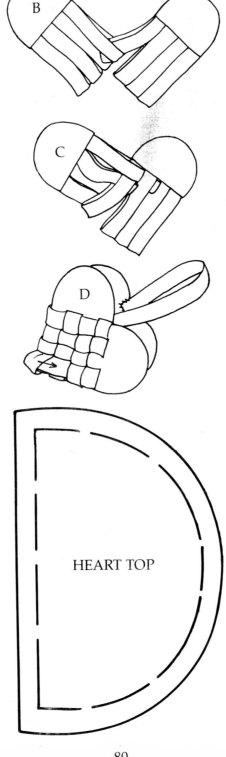

HEART TOP

Bird Ornaments

Note: Before beginning, read General Directions for Painting on Fabric on page 20.

SKILL LEVEL: Intermediate

MATERIALS: Muslin. Fiberfill. Thread. Graphite paper. Acrylic paint: white, yellow, orange, brown, black. Rapidograph pen. Rice grass with stalks. Gold pearl cotton for hanging.

DIRECTIONS: Trace patterns and quilting lines for two bodies and four wings for each bird; reverse patterns for duplicate pieces. Using graphite paper, transfer all lines to right side of each muslin piece. Cut out bodies and wings. Sew body pieces with marked sides together, leaving opening for turning; turn to right side and stuff with fiberfill until firm. Slip-stitch opening closed. Sew pairs of wing pieces together in same manner, stuffing lightly and evenly with fiberfill after turning. Machine-quilt along quilting lines. Bend wings slightly and slip-stitch to sides of bodies.

Paint birds following photographs. For "sparrow," paint beak yellow; paint eye black with a white highlight. Paint sparrow's body brown and gray with light brown highlights; paint wings black and brown with yellow highlights. For "oriole," paint breast orange, red, and yellow; paint beak white. Paint body in shades of black and dark gray; paint wings black, with red highlights in shaded areas. After painting, draw feathers and highlight feature lines with rapidograph pen.

For legs, cut four 1" stalks from rice grass; glue grass at tips for feet. Glue legs to each side of bird at placement line. Attach pearl cotton at top for hanging.

ADAPTATION: Make four or five birds of your choice and hang from dowels for mobile.

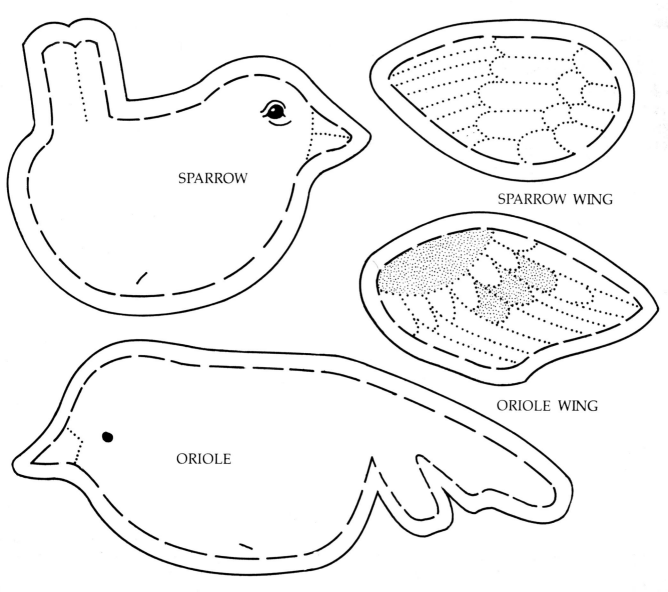

SPARROW

SPARROW WING

ORIOLE WING

ORIOLE

Treetop Gnomes and Star

Note: Before beginning, read General Directions for Soft Sculpture Head on page 18.

SKILL LEVEL: Advanced

MATERIALS: *For Bodies:* Medium-weight muslin, 45" wide, ½ yard. Fiberfill. White fake fur with at least 1½" nap. Acrylic paint: white, red, yellow, blue, steel gray, burnt sienna. Brown felt-tipped fine line marking pen. String. *For Clothes:* Cotton fabric, 45" wide, ¼ yard each: hunter green, beige; ⅛ yard blue; scrap maroon. Scrap olive/brown wool fabric. Scraps felt: red, gray. Scrap gold velveteen or fake suede. Matching thread. Small gold buckle. Maroon six-strand embroidery floss. Gray fake fur with short nap. *For Star:* Cotton fabric, 45" wide, ⅛ yard each: bright yellow, yellow gingham. Yellow grosgrain ribbon, ⅜" wide, 1 yard. ¼" elastic, 5".

DIRECTIONS: *Bodies:* Cut 7"-diameter circle from muslin for each head. Trace patterns and use to cut two noses. Cut out two 1¼" circles from muslin for

male's ears. Trace patterns and use to cut out wig for female gnome, and beard and ¾ x 3" strip of hair for male gnome, from white fake fur. Complete heads following directions on page 18.

Trace patterns and use to cut two arms, four legs, and two foot soles for each gnome from muslin. Sew arms together so you have a right and left arm for each. Sew two pairs of legs together along front and back seams, then stitch sole to opening at bottom. Turn arms and legs to right side and stuff very firmly with fiberfill; paint flesh.

To make bodies, cut an 11 x 6" piece of muslin for female and 8 x 5" piece for male. Sew 6" edges of female's body and 5" edges of male's body together, making two tubes; turn to right side. Baste around top and bottom edges of each tube. Pull basting tightly at one end (top) of each; tie off and push raw edges inside. Pull basting at other end of each slightly, then fill pouches with fiberfill to medium firmness. Pull and tie off basting at bottom, enclosing fiberfill; push raw edges inside. Slip-stitch head to top, legs to bottom, and arms to sides of body about ¾" below neck. For female, mold body so bosom area is about 7" around, and derriere area is about 9". Tie a string around waist (about halfway up body), making waist measurement 6½". Male's body is not contoured, but should be approximately the same height as female's.

Clothes for Female: Trace patterns and use to mark two kerchiefs, two blouses, and two sleeves on beige fabric; do not cut out. Trace patterns and use to cut two cuffs and one neckband from maroon fabric. Cut one 7 x 1½" waistband and one 23 x 6" skirt from hunter green fabric. Trace patterns and use to cut four gray fur boot uppers and two gray felt soles; also cut one gray felt cap.

Following *General Directions for Embroidery* on page 18, trans-

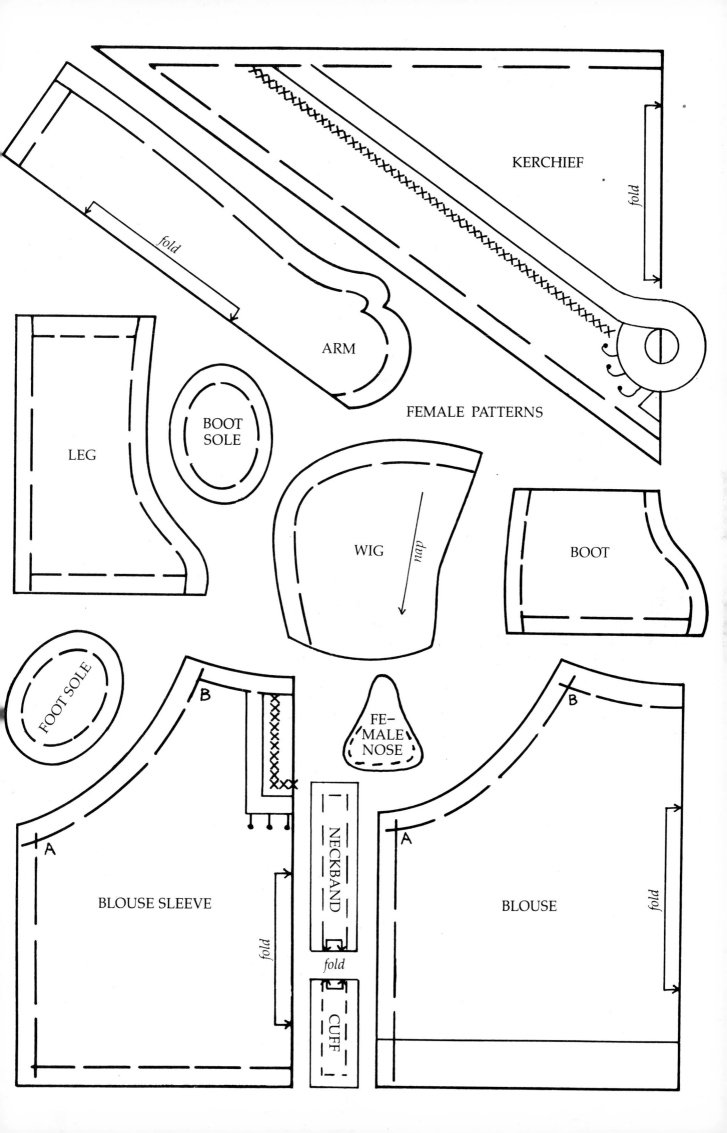

KERCHIEF

fold

ARM

FEMALE PATTERNS

LEG

BOOT
SOLE

WIG

nap

BOOT

FOOT SOLE

FE-
MALE
NOSE

B

A

B

NECKBAND

fold

A

BLOUSE SLEEVE

fold

fold

CUFF

BLOUSE

fold

fer embroidery lines to right sides of one kerchief and two sleeves. Using three strands of floss in needle, embroider all X's in cross stitch, all dots in French knots, all lines extending from dots in straight stitch, and all other lines in chain stitch (see Embroidery Stitch Details, page 18). Cut out clothing pieces when embroidery is completed.

Sew kerchief pieces together with right sides facing and raw edges even, leaving opening for turning; turn to right side and slip-stitch opening closed. Press, then wrap kerchief around female's head; slip-stitch ends at back. Make cap following directions on page 20; slip-stitch to head over kerchief.

Cut one blouse piece in half for blouse back. Sew raglan sleeves to blouse front and back between A and B on pattern with right sides facing and raw edges even, then machine-baste around neck edge and bottom edge of each sleeve. Press one long edge of neckband and each cuff ⅛" to wrong side. With right sides facing and raw edges even gather neck edge to fit neck-band, gather sleeves to fit each cuff, and sew together at raw edges. Sew side seams of blouse, continuing sewing to ends of cuffs. Fold neckband and cuffs to wrong side; slip-stitch pressed edges over seam-line. Fold raw edges at back of blouse ¼" to wrong side; slip-stitch and press. Slip blouse onto gnome; sew back edges together, overlapping edges about ½". Stuff front of blouse with fiberfill to simulate the female gnome's ample bosom.

For skirt, sew 6" edges of skirt together with right sides facing and raw edges even, making tube; end stitching 1½" away from one (top) edge. Baste around top edge; make 2" hem at bottom. Press one long edge of waistband ¼" to wrong side; gather skirt to fit waistband, and sew together along raw edges. Press and sew raw edges at opening ¼" to wrong side, then finish waistband same as

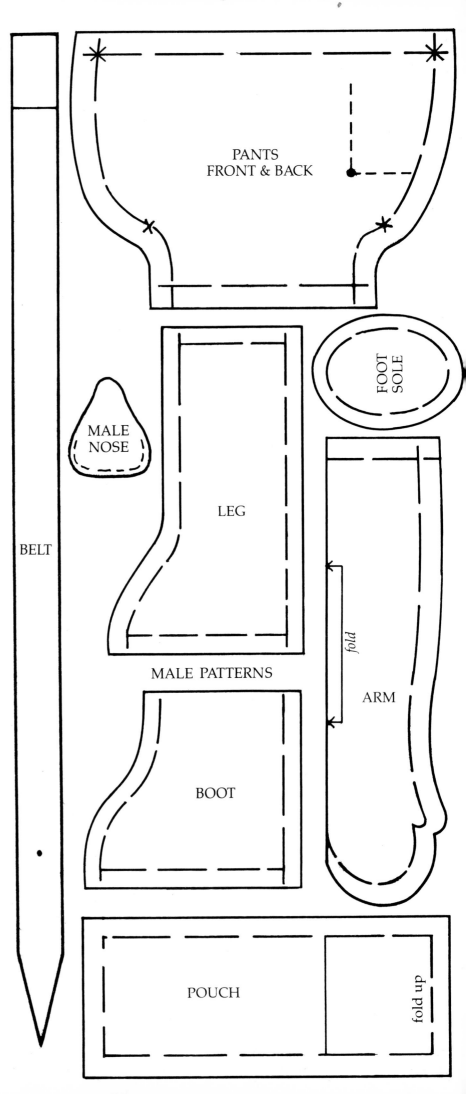

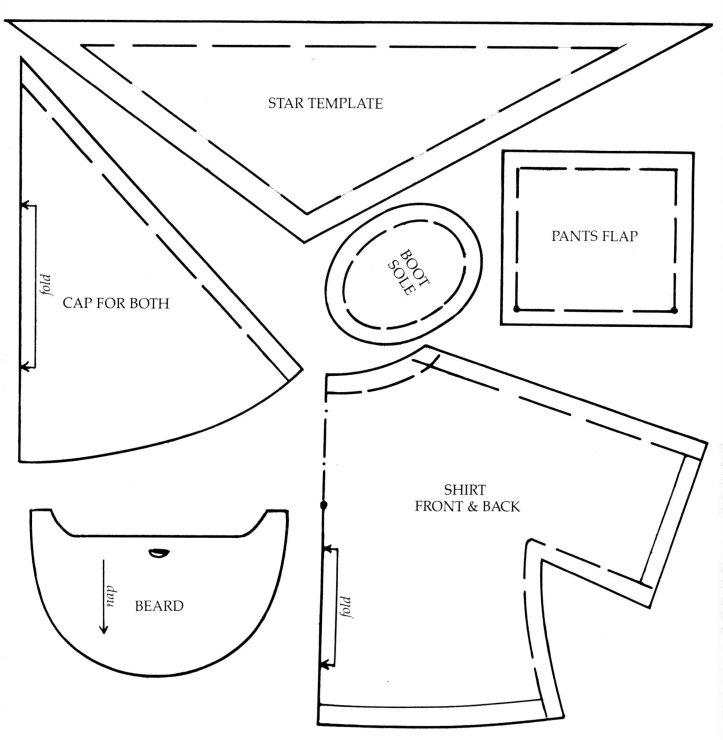

STAR TEMPLATE

PANTS FLAP

CAP FOR BOTH

fold

BOOT SOLE

SHIRT FRONT & BACK

fold

BEARD

nap

for neckband. Turn skirt to right side. Place skirt on gnome, overlapping ends of waistband about ½"; slip-stitch waistband so it fits gnome snugly and holds fiberfill bosom in place.

Sew front and back edges of boot uppers together with right sides facing and raw edges even, then stitch sole to bottom of each. Turn to right side. Pull boots onto gnome's feet, and tack in place. Fold gnome's hands together at front; slip-stitch to secure.

Clothing for Male: Trace and use patterns to cut one shirt front and one shirt back from blue fabric; one pants front, one

pants back, and two flaps from olive/brown wool; cap from red felt.

Make cap following directions on page 20, and slip-stitch to head. Clip shirt front down to dot. Sew shirt front and back together with right sides facing and raw edges even at shoulders and side seams; turn to right side. Make a ¼" hem at shirt bottom and sleeves. Press raw edges at shirt front and neck ¼" to wrong side, clipping curves as necessary; topstitch in place. Place shirt on gnome.

Sew pants front and back together along sides between X's with raw edges even. Fold,

matching sewn seams, and sew inside of legs and crotch. Turn pants inside out. Fold and sew raw edges at waist, and hem ¼" to inside. Sew flap pieces together, leaving opening for turning. Turn inside out; slip-stitch opening closed. Place pants on gnome; make pleat in front to take up excess fabric; slip-stitch in place. Slip-stitch flap over pleat. Make boots same as for female; place on feet, stuffing bottom of pants legs into boots.

Trace patterns and use to cut one belt and two pouches from gold velveteen. Attach buckle to one end of belt; make a hole in belt as indicated. Place belt on male so it is about ⅜" above hem of shirt. For pouch, sew pieces together with right sides facing and raw edges even, leaving opening for turning. Turn to right side and slip-stitch opening closed. Following pattern, fold along line and slip-stitch sides together. Fold remaining piece down for flap; tack. Slip belt through pouch and buckle closed. Bring hands behind gnome and slip-stitch in place.

Star: Trace template for half-diamond and use to cut five bright yellow and five yellow gingham pieces for each star. Sew pieces together along center seam line, forming five diamond shapes, half bright yellow and half yellow gingham. Sew diamond shapes together along short sides, alternating fabrics as shown in *Star Diagram,* forming a star; press. Repeat to make star back. Sew stars together with right sides facing and raw edges even, leaving opening for turning. Turn to right side; stuff with fiberfill until firm, then slip-stitch opening closed.

Cut elastic in half; sew ends of each piece together, forming two loops. Sew loops securely to one side of star near center, spaced about 3" apart and directly in line with one another; loops attach star to top of tree. Slip-stitch middle of ribbon to center of front side of star. Attach ribbon ends to gnomes' hands.

STAR DIAGRAM

ADAPTATION: Reduce size of star and use as tree ornament.

Christmas Tree Skirt

Note: Before beginning, read General Directions for Appliqué on page 17.

SKILL LEVEL: Intermediate

MATERIALS: Cotton fabric, 45" wide: white, 1⅜ yards; kelly green polka dot, 1½ yards; red, hunter green, ½ yard each. White ruffled eyelet trim, ¾" wide, 5 yards. Hunter green extra-wide double-fold bias seam tape. Velcro fastening strip, ½ yard. Batting. White quilting thread. Thread to match fabrics. Paper for patterns. String. Thumbtack. Pencil. Scissors. Graphite paper.

DIRECTIONS: Make compass using thumbtack, pencil, and 22½" length of string. Tack end of string to center of 46" square sheet of paper; tack other end to pencil. Swing pencil around to mark circle 45" in diameter. Mark second circle 4" in diameter in center of large circle. Use scallop pattern to mark scallops all around edge of outer circle. Adjust scallops to even them out if necessary. Draw line from point of one scallop to center point of circle. Cut out center circle and along drawn line; cut around scalloped circle. Use pattern to cut one white skirt and one green polka dot backing. From white, also cut facing 20 x 3" for skirt slit; press one long edge of facing ¼" to wrong side. Sew long raw edge of facing to one edge of skirt slit with right sides together. Zigzag-stitch male half of Velcro to facing, flush with seamline.

Enlarge, trace, and complete half-pattern for appliqué design, following the photograph above. Transfer four complete designs to white fabric, spaced evenly apart and with center of each heart 8" away from scalloped edge of skirt using graphite paper. Use pattern to cut pieces for four appliqué designs: cut heart from red fabric; four large center leaves from hunter green; and small outer leaves from green polka dot fabric. Machine-appliqué pieces to skirt in marked positions. With

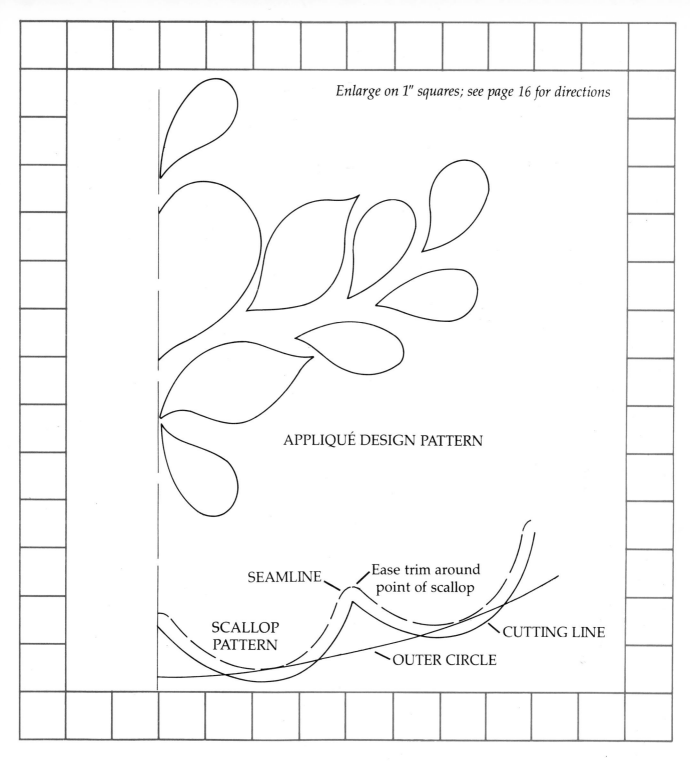

Enlarge on 1" squares; see page 16 for directions

APPLIQUÉ DESIGN PATTERN

SEAMLINE

Ease trim around
point of scallop

SCALLOP
PATTERN

CUTTING LINE

OUTER CIRCLE

raw edges even, sew ruffled eyelet trim to right side of white skirt, easing trim around points of scallops.

Place appliquéd skirt, wrong side up, on large flat surface. Position batting over skirt; trim ¼" smaller at all edges; baste in place. With right sides facing, raw edges even, and trim in between, sew backing to appliquéd skirt around scalloped edges and along straight edge without facing; do not sew along edge with facing. Clip curves and point of each scallop; turn tree skirt to right side. Baste skirt horizontally, vertically, and around inner circle.

Fold facing over to backing side; slip-stitch in place. Fold ends of facing at scalloped edge inside; slip-stitch in place. Slip-stitch female Velcro strip to backing along edge opposite facing; do not let stitches show on right side. Sandwich raw edges of inner circle with seam tape; sew in place, enclosing raw edges.

Hand-quilt tree skirt 1" away from scalloped edge all around, so quilting resembles a scallop pattern; also quilt ⅛" away from each appliqué. Remove all basting.

ADAPTATIONS: Do not mark or cut inner circle or slit; leave

opening for turning along scalloped edge. Complete as for tree skirt but use as tea skirt. Paint design rather than appliqué.

The children are usually tired, but too
excited to sleep. After getting ready for
bed, they rush to the den where John
waits by the fire to read them *The Night
Before Christmas*. Then we bring out the
Family Christmas Book, and each person
makes an entry – some thoughts or perhaps a drawing. Before heading upstairs,
the children leave a reminder for Santa
on the mantel, set out his cookies and
milk, and make sure there is porridge
in the kitchen for our gnomes....

Toothbrush Gnome and Soap Dish

SKILL LEVEL: Elementary

MATERIALS: Commercially prepared low-fire porcelain clay. Transparent overglaze. Cones for firing (*see package directions for cone numbers*). Damp cloth. Two ¼"-thick lattice strips. Rolling pin. Bowl of water. Sponge. Sturdy cardboard. Trimming needle. Kiln. Brush for glaze.

DIRECTIONS: Roll clay into ¼"-thick slab as follows: Place clay on damp cloth stretched between two lattice strips on work surface. Keep ends of rolling pin on lattice strips while flattening clay to insure an even thickness. Roll from center of clay outward, moving lattice strips as necessary. Wash rolling pin occasionally and wipe dry to prevent clay from sticking. Make sure flattened clay slab is free from cracks or tears.

Make cardboard template of both pattern pieces; position templates on clay slab. Cut around templates with trimming needle to cut out shapes; allow clay to stiffen slightly before removing excess to prevent stretching cut shapes.

For toothbrush holder, use trimming needle to bore hole for hanging in tip of cap as indicated on pattern. While clay is fairly damp, bend form along dot/dash line at waist and prop against a wall to harden in that position. Bend hands forward and around along dot/dash lines to hold toothbrushes. Bend feet up along dot/dash lines.

For soap dish, follow dot/dash lines on pattern and place bar of soap in center of leaf. While clay is fairly damp, bend edges of leaf up around soap and outward following *Soap Dish Diagram*. Bend stem into an inverted "J" as shown.

ADAPTATION: Use pattern for *Female Painted Gnome Cookie* on page 43 to make female toothbrush holder.

See patterns on following page

91

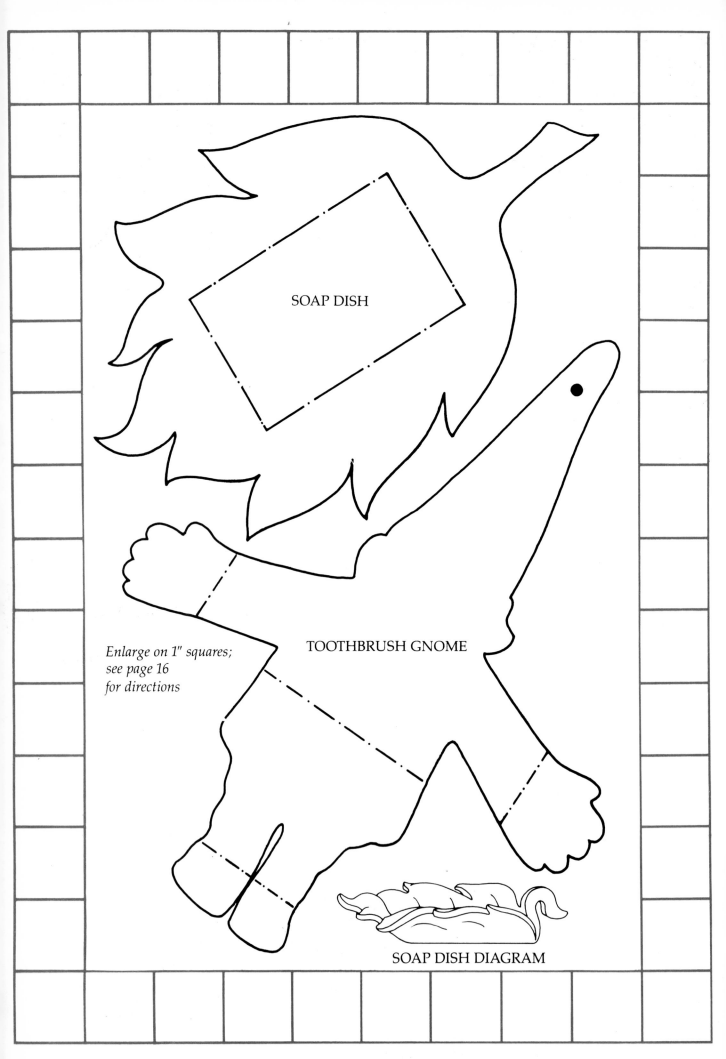

SOAP DISH

TOOTHBRUSH GNOME

Enlarge on 1" squares; see page 16 for directions

SOAP DISH DIAGRAM

TOOTHBRUSH GNOME & SOAP DISH PATTERNS

Gnome Soap and Soap Box

SKILL LEVEL: Elementary

MATERIALS: *For Soap:* Bar of your favorite soap. Scissors. Wax. Double boiler for melting wax. Tongs. *For Soap Box:* ¼" basswood, two 4 x 22" sheets. Sharp pencil. Cork-backed steel ruler. Jig or coping saw. Brads. Hammer. Glue. Sandpaper. White acrylic paint. Medium paintbrush. Spray sealer.

DIRECTIONS: *Soap:* Cut prints of your choice from page 153. Melt wax in double boiler. Wet back of print with water and apply to one side of soap; print will adhere. Using tongs, dip print side of soap into wax; do not dip entire bar of soap. Allow to cool.

Soap Box: Mark the following pieces on basswood using sharp pencil and cork-backed steel ruler: one door and one bottom, each 7¼ x 3½"; two sides, 7¼ x 2¼"; one doorstop, 1 x 7¼"; two ends, 4 x 2¼". Cut gnome print from page 153 and glue to scrap of basswood for handle. Cut out all pieces (including handle piece) using jig or coping saw; sand until smooth.

To assemble box, glue bottom between side pieces; glue ends to bottom and side pieces with edges flush. Insert doorstop into box and glue to one side piece ¼" below top edge. Let glue dry; nail doorstop with brads to secure. Using sandpaper, sand one long edge of door so edge becomes rounded. Glue gnome handle next to unsanded edge, centered between top and bottom; let glue dry thoroughly. Insert door into box so handle is on same side as doorstop. "Hinge" door into box as follows: holding door so it is flush with top edges of side and end pieces, drive brads through end pieces and into door close to sanded edge.

Seal all wood surfaces inside and out; when dry, paint entire box white, painting carefully around handle. Seal again after paint dries.

ADAPTATION: Paint box as desired and line with colorful fabric or paper.

A male gnome likes to bathe upon waking and before breakfast. His wife prepares the bath.

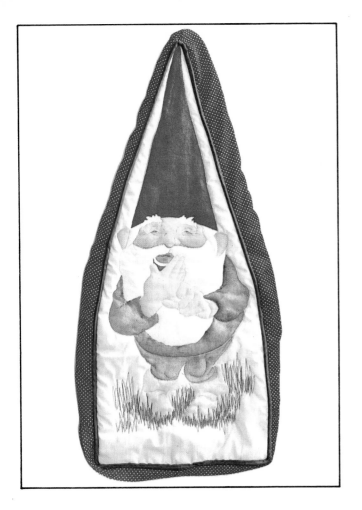

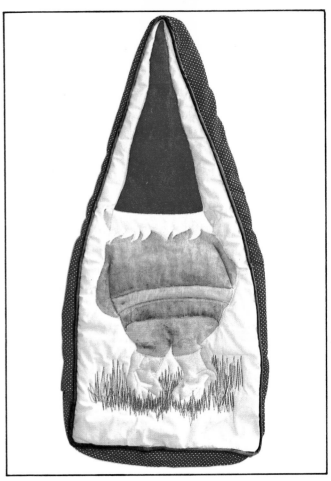

Pajama Pillow

Note: Before beginning, read General Directions for Painting on Fabric on page 20.

SKILL LEVEL: Intermediate

MATERIALS: Muslin, 45″ wide, ¾ yard. Red polka dot cotton fabric, 45″ wide, ½ yard. Green piping, 3⅓ yards. White 22″ skirt zipper. Batting. Matching thread. Acrylic paint: red, white, yellow, blue, gold, brown, gray. Rapidograph pen. Graphite paper.

DIRECTIONS: Enlarge pattern as indicated opposite. Trace and use outline of pillow to cut four pieces from muslin. Transfer design for gnome front to one piece of muslin and design for gnome back to another using graphite paper and dry ballpoint pen. Insert layer of batting between marked and unmarked muslin pieces for back and front; trim to match. Baste three layers of each together horizontally, vertically, and diagonally, making two padded pieces.

Paint gnome front and back following photograph. Mix red with brown for tongue; shade pink cheeks just above moustache. Using rapidograph pen, highlight gnome's features and fill in eyes. Machine-quilt following each outline of design (including face) using white thread. Using green thread, machine-embroider all around gnome's feet with random stitch to simulate grass (*see General Directions for Embroidery, page 18*).

Pin piping to marked side of both front and back pieces, matching sewing line on piping to seam allowance line on muslin; sew in place. To end piping, cut ½″ of cord out of one end, turn edges of empty fabric tube to inside, and insert opposite end into opening.

Cut a 45 x 3″ strip from red polka dot fabric; press each short end ½″ to wrong side. Begin pinning strip at one X on gnome front with right sides facing, raw edges even, and piping in between. Continue pinning strip around top of gnome, easing fabric at tip of cap, and ending at opposite X. Using zipper foot, and with piping as a guide, sew polka dot strip in place along marked seamline. To connect front and back, place back piece over front with right sides facing and raw edges even. Pin back to polka dot strip from X to X, and machine sew as for front

Cut two 2 x 22″ strips from red polka dot fabric. Machine-baste strips together ½″ from one long edge with right sides facing and raw edges even. Press seam open. Lay zipper with zipper pull facing and centered on wrong side of seam. Pin zipper in place. Sew zipper to fabric following sewing lines. Remove basting. Pin zipper piece to back and front of gnome at bottom with right sides facing and raw edges even; fabric will overlap other strip at X's. Sew in place, connecting front to back. Open zipper and turn to right side.

ADAPTATION: Stuff with fiberfill.

94

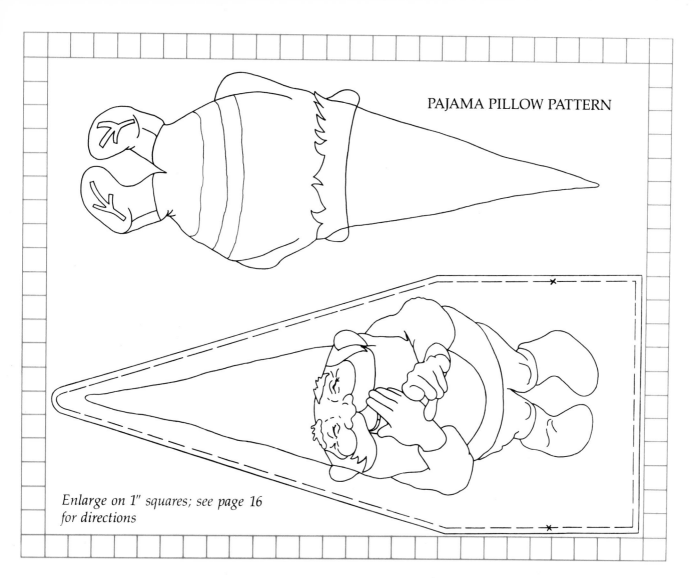

PAJAMA PILLOW PATTERN

Enlarge on 1" squares; see page 16 for directions

When a gnome bathes, he puts a couple of handfuls of dried soapwort in the water to produce an abundance of suds.

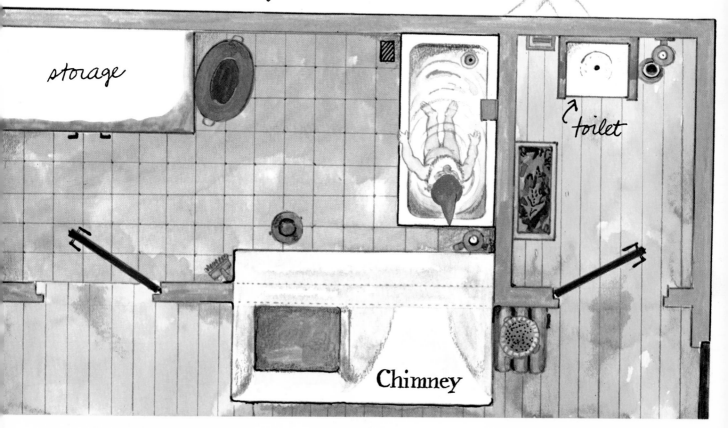

sewer

storage

toilet

Chimney

Doorknob Gnome

Note: Before beginning, read General Directions for Painting on Fabric on page 20.

SKILL LEVEL: Intermediate

MATERIALS: Muslin, ¼ yard. Fiberfill. Scrap red felt. Spring-action clothespin. Acrylic paint: white, red, yellow, blue, gray, gold, brown. Rapidograph pen. ¼" elastic, 4" long. Graphite paper.

DIRECTIONS: Trace and transfer patterns for front, back, four arms, and four legs (reverse patterns for two arms and two legs) to muslin using graphite paper. Paint muslin following photograph. Let paint dry. Outline and highlight painted areas with rapidograph pen, paying special attention to details in face.

Cut out pieces. Sew two pairs of arms and two pairs of legs together along curved edges with raw edges even, leaving openings for turning. Turn to right side and stuff with fiberfill; slip-stitch openings closed. With raw edges even, sew arms to body front between X's so arms curve downward. Sew body front to body back, with right sides facing and raw edges even, sewing over arms to secure them in place and leaving bottom open for turning. Turn to right side and hand-baste around bottom of body; stuff with fiberfill, pushing fiberfill to tip of cap. Flatten tops of legs so seams and X's match. Insert legs into bottom of body, matching X's. Pull basting, gathering body to fit around legs. Slip-stitch legs in place, making sure all raw edges of body are tucked inside.

Draw bird tracks on the bottom of each foot with rapidograph pen. Glue two fluffs of fiberfill on gnome's face for eyebrows. Trace pattern and use to cut cap front and back from red felt; glue in place on gnome's head; whip-stitch side edges. Slip-stitch ends of elastic to derriere, making a loop. Paint clothespin white. Let paint dry. Glue hands over top edges of clothespin as shown in photograph. Attach gnome to doorknob with elastic.

ADAPTATIONS: Hang gnome on fire screen with reversible sign reading "Damper Open/Damper Closed." Use to hold phone messages or recipes.

See following page for additional patterns

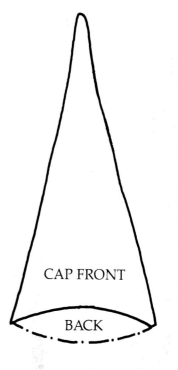

CAP FRONT

BACK

97

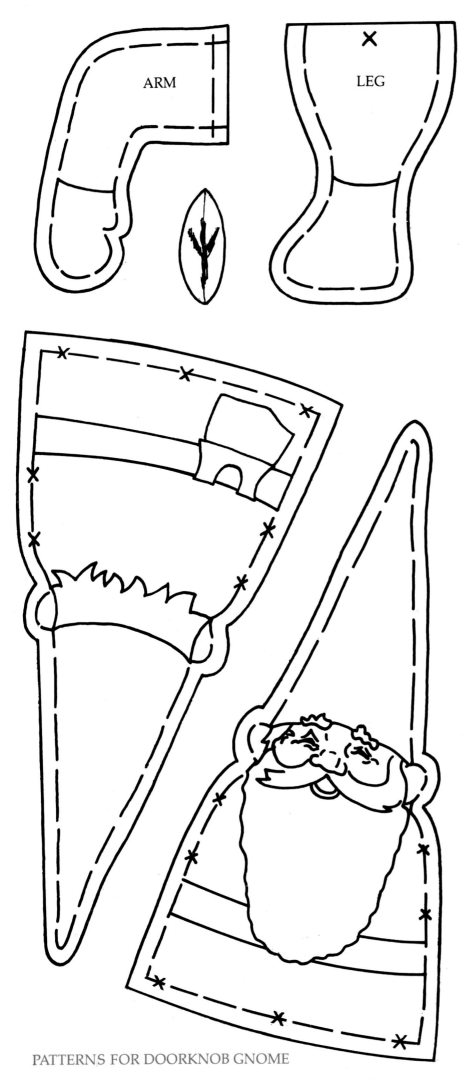

ARM

LEG

PATTERNS FOR DOORKNOB GNOME

Gnome Puzzle and Gift Tags

SKILL LEVEL: Elementary

MATERIALS: ¼" basswood. Jig or coping saw. Drill with ¼" bit. Acrylic paint: white, gold, desired colors for flowers and leaves. Pearl cotton. Grosgrain ribbon. Acrylic varnish. Medium paintbrush.

DIRECTIONS: *Puzzle:* Cut out prints for gnome front and back from page 153. Glue front to basswood; allow to dry thoroughly. Using jig or coping saw, carefully cut around outline of gnome; drill small hole between legs and cut out space between legs. Glue back print to other side of wood, lining up edges. Trim where necessary. Use jig or coping saw to cut wood into puzzle pieces following dot/dash lines on *Puzzle Diagram*. Apply one coat acrylic varnish and let dry. Put puzzle in bag of your choice *(see page 40).*

Gift Tags (may be used as ornaments): Cut out desired prints from page 153 or from decorative paper. Using jig or coping saw cut desired-size ovals, circles, or squares from basswood; drill hole near one edge for hanging. Paint basswood white or desired color. Glue print to center of one side of each piece. Paint design of your choice, or "To" and "From," on back of wood using acrylic paint.

Or, cut out print from page 153 and glue to wood, then cut out around shape. Drill small hole at top for hanging. Paint side edges gold and back side white. Paint message of your choice on back.

Varnish ornament or tag, back and front. Thread pearl cotton or ribbon through hole for hanging.

ADAPTATIONS: Use tag on key chain, as pet tag, or as zipper pull. Use favorite picture or print for puzzle instead of gnome print.

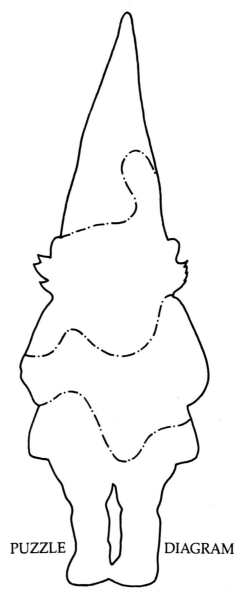

PUZZLE DIAGRAM

99

Merry Christmas Kids

Note: Before beginning, read General Directions for Appliqué on page 17.

SKILL LEVEL: Intermediate

MATERIALS: Cotton jersey knit fabric, 60" wide, ⅓ yard each: pink, blue, white. Felt, 72" wide, ¼ yard each: red, green. Yellow knitting worsted-weight yarn. Acrylic paint: blue, pink. Grosgrain ribbon, ⅜" wide: 2⅓ yards red; 2½ yards hunter green. Cotton fabric, 45" wide: 1¼ yards red polka dot; ⅝ yard green gingham with ⅛" check; ⅓ yard white with strawberry print. Six-strand embroidery floss, 4 skeins hunter green. Fiberfill. Red pearl cotton. Two 1"-diameter red beads. Red double-fold bias seam tape, 4 yards. Thread to match fabrics. Compass. Thin, stiff cardboard for patterns. Twelve ½"-diameter metal forms for fabric-covered buttons. Rouge.

DIRECTIONS: *For Kids:* Trace patterns for body; make separate patterns for front (entire outline) and bottom (lower section). Use compass to mark 6"-diameter circle for head pattern. Transfer patterns to thin, stiff cardboard; coat edges of cardboard patterns with nail polish to prevent fraying. Place cardboard patterns on fabric and trace around them to mark one front, one back, one bottom, and four sleeves for each of six girls on pink fabric and for each of six boys on blue fabric; mark one head and four hands on white fabric for each. Cut out along marked lines.

Make each of six girls and six boys as follows: Baste 1" away from edge of head; pull basting, gathering circle slightly, and fill center of circle with fiberfill. Pull basting tight when head is medium-firm and tie off enclosing fiberfill. Make a nose by covering metal button form with white fabric. Slip-stitch

button nose to head 2½" above tied-off neck. Paint smiling mouth with pink acrylic paint; paint two blue eyes. Rub rouge on cheeks.

Sew back to bottom between A and B, easing back to fit; sew pieced back to front with right sides facing and raw edges even, leaving top open between dots. Clip curves; turn to right side and stuff with fiberfill until firm. Insert tied-off neck into opening of body; slip-stitch together securely, pushing all raw edges inside body. Sew one hand to each sleeve with raw straight edges even. Sew two pairs of arms together with raw edges even, leaving opening for turning; turn to right side and stuff with fiberfill. Push raw edges inside and slip-stitch opening closed. Slip-stitch arms to body, matching X's for placement. For boy, cut about 25 lengths of yellow yarn, 1½" long; glue to head for hair. Trace pattern and use to cut red cap. Sew seam, turn to right side, and slip-stitch to boy's head. For girl, cut 20 lengths of yellow yarn, 10" long; drape in a bunch

across top of head, and slip-stitch from front to back for center part. Braid each side starting at cheek; tack braid to each side of head. Cut two 6" lengths of red ribbon; tie a bow around bottom of each braid. Use pattern to cut green cap; make same as for boy's cap and slip-stitch to top of girl's head.

For Pillows: Trace separate patterns for pillow and heart (add ¼" seam allowance). Transfer outline of each to cardboard. Use cardboard patterns to mark 30 pillow pieces on white fabric with strawberries and 15 heart pieces on red polka dot fabric. Trace letters spelling "Merry Christmas" and transfer each letter outline to all but one heart using graphite paper. Using four strands of hunter green floss in needle, embroider letters in satin stitch following *Embroidery Stitch Detail* on page 18. When embroidery is completed, cut out all pillow and heart pieces along marked lines.

Using green thread, machine-appliqué one heart to center of each of 15 pillows using zigzag satin stitch. For pillow ruffles,

cut 15 strips, each 22½ x 2½", from gingham. Sew short ends of each together, making 15 circles. Fold each circle in half with raw edges of seam inside; machine-baste around raw edges. Pull basting, gathering one ruffle to fit each appliquéd pillow. Sew ruffle to pillow with raw edges even (folded edge of ruffle faces center of pillow), easing fabric around corners. Sew plain pillow pieces to each appliquéd front with right sides facing raw edges even, and ruffle in between, leaving opening for turning. Turn to right side; stuff with fiberfill until plump, then slip-stitch opening closed.

Cut 15 lengths of hunter green ribbon, each 6" long; tie each into a bow. Tack bow to each pillow front at position marked by X.

For Mantel Skirt: Cut three 45 x 11½" pieces from red polka dot fabric (or measure 1½ times the width of your mantel). Sew pieces together along 11½" edges, making one long strip. Hem top, bottom, and side edges by turning fabric under ¼" twice and sewing in place. Measure 1¾" below top long edge; mark a line parallel to long edge along length of fabric on wrong side. Center bias seam tape over this line and top-stitch

long edges of seam tape in place for casing. Cut length of red pearl cotton the width of your mantel plus 10"; run through casing using safety pin to gather the fabric. Attach beads to ends of pearl cotton. Tack mantel cover across top of mantel; arrange gnomes and pillows behind cover as shown in photograph.

ADAPTATIONS: Make up your own message instead of "Merry Christmas." Appliqué mantel skirt as desired using any appliqué motif in book. Thread gnome kids hand-in-hand across baby's crib.

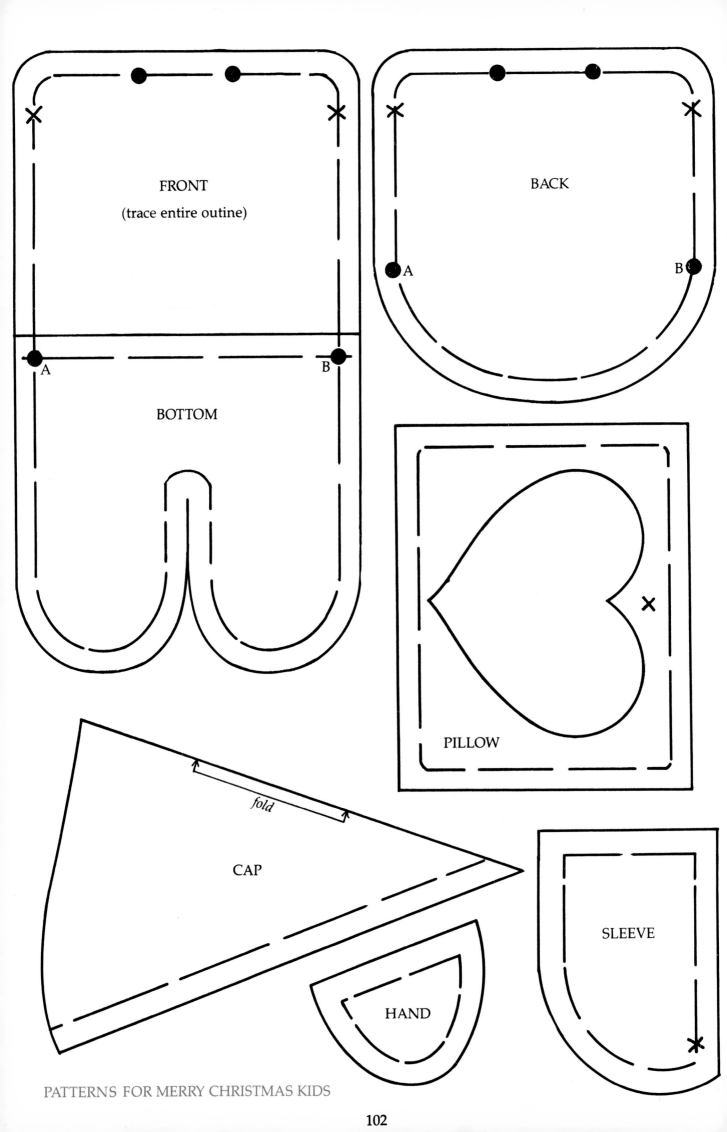

FRONT
(trace entire outine)

BACK

A

B

A

B

BOTTOM

PILLOW

fold

CAP

SLEEVE

HAND

PATTERNS FOR MERRY CHRISTMAS KIDS

Climbing Gnome

Note: Before beginning, read General Directions for Woodworking on page 16 for additional materials and directions.

SKILL LEVEL: Elementary

MATERIALS: ¾" wood, such as walnut or mahogany, about 12" square. Drill with ¼" bit. Furniture wax. Red macramé cord, about 4 yards. Three large wooden beads.

DIRECTIONS: Mark ¾ x 8" bar on wood, then trace and transfer outline of climbing gnome to remaining portion of wood. Using jig or coping saw, cut out pieces along marked lines.

Drill holes at an angle through gnome's hands following dash lines on pattern. On bar, drill hole in center, then drill one hole 2½" away from center on each side. Sand pieces until smooth; dust with tack cloth. Rub pieces with furniture wax for a lustrous finish.

Cut 7"-length of cord; insert through center hole. Knot one end into loop for hanging; knot other end around bead. Cut two pieces of cord of equal length as desired; insert through side holes on bar. Knot at top (same side as loop); draw other ends through gnome's hands, top to bottom, then knot ends around beads. Hang climbing gnome from loop, then pull each bead in turn to make gnome climb up cords.

ADAPTATION: Cut out animal shape instead of gnome, being sure to angle holes.

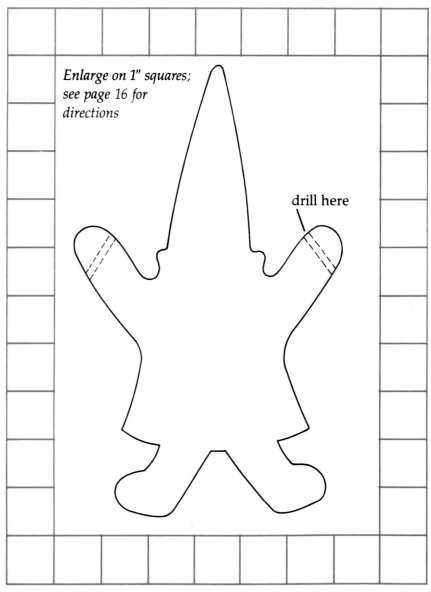

Enlarge on 1" squares; see page 16 for directions

drill here

The bedroom is cold and the children snuggle beneath the Christmas quilt for warmth. We allow them to start out together in our bed – a treat that is saved for Christmas Eve.

John and I return to the living room to place a few surprise ornaments on the tree. We fill its boughs with slices of candied fruit, chocolate rings with colored sprinkles, and a menagerie of marzipan animals. Finally we settle down to some tea, a few leftover cookies, and the wrapping of some last-minute gifts.

Now is the time when we exchange our own presents and discuss the upcoming Family Christmas Pageant. Everyone will take part. Grandpa Endler will read aloud <u>The Little Match Girl</u> (we cry each time we hear it). Grandma Endler will tell tales of the little <u>tonttu</u> (gnomes) who lived in her village in Finland. And John and I will lead the family musicians and direct the children in their skit. This year they will reenact the story of the Three Kings, with a supporting cast of family and friends.

And of course there will be singing.

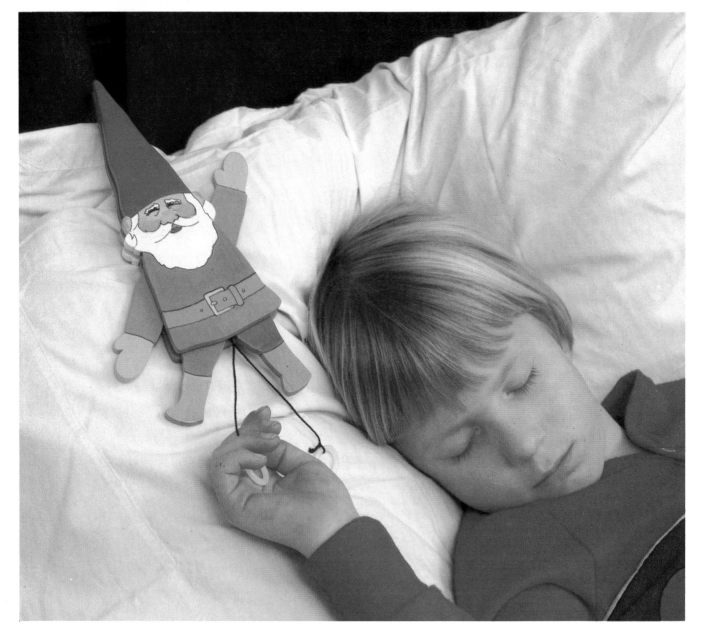

Dancing Gnome Marionette

Note: Before beginning, read General Directions for Woodworking on page 16 for additional materials and directions.

SKILL LEVEL: Intermediate

MATERIALS: ¼" basswood, one 4 x 22" sheet. ⅛" dowel, 2" long; ⅜" dowel, ¼" long. Acrylic paint: colors listed in *Color Key*. Rapidograph pen. Black pearl cotton. Two plastic rings, about ¾" in diameter. White glue. Clear drying varnish. Drill with ¾" and ¹⁄₁₆" bits. Medium paintbrushes. Graphite paper.

DIRECTIONS: Trace patterns for gnome front, back, two arms, and two legs; transfer outlines only to basswood. Cut out using jig or coping saw. Mark exact positions for holes on wrong sides of front and back pieces following *Back* and *Front Drilling Diagrams*. Using ⅛" bit, drill four holes ⅛" deep into each piece; also drill holes all the way through arm and leg pieces in positions indicated by black dots. Using ¹⁄₁₆" bit, drill holes through side edges of wood on arm and leg pieces following dash lines. Sand; dust with tack cloth. Transfer design onto all pieces using graphite paper; features are later highlighted with rapidograph pen.

Paint both sides of all pieces following *Color Key*; for side edges and wrong sides of body front and back pieces, paint red hat, flesh ears, white hair, and blue body, matching design lines and colors on front and back of body. For rosy face and ears, mix red with white and blend onto face just above beard and at tips of ears; let dry. Mark all design lines with rapidograph pen. Varnish pieces.

Cut four ½"-long pieces from ⅛" dowel; whittle ends of each if necessary to fit into drilled holes on body pieces. Glue dowels into holes on back piece. Paint ⅜" dowel red; glue to back piece, same side as other dowels, centered near tip of cap. Cut two 9" lengths pearl cotton; thread through arms and legs following *Threading Diagram*. Knot thread as shown and attach rings to free ends. Position arms and legs over dowels, then attach front body piece. Pull strings to make gnome dance.

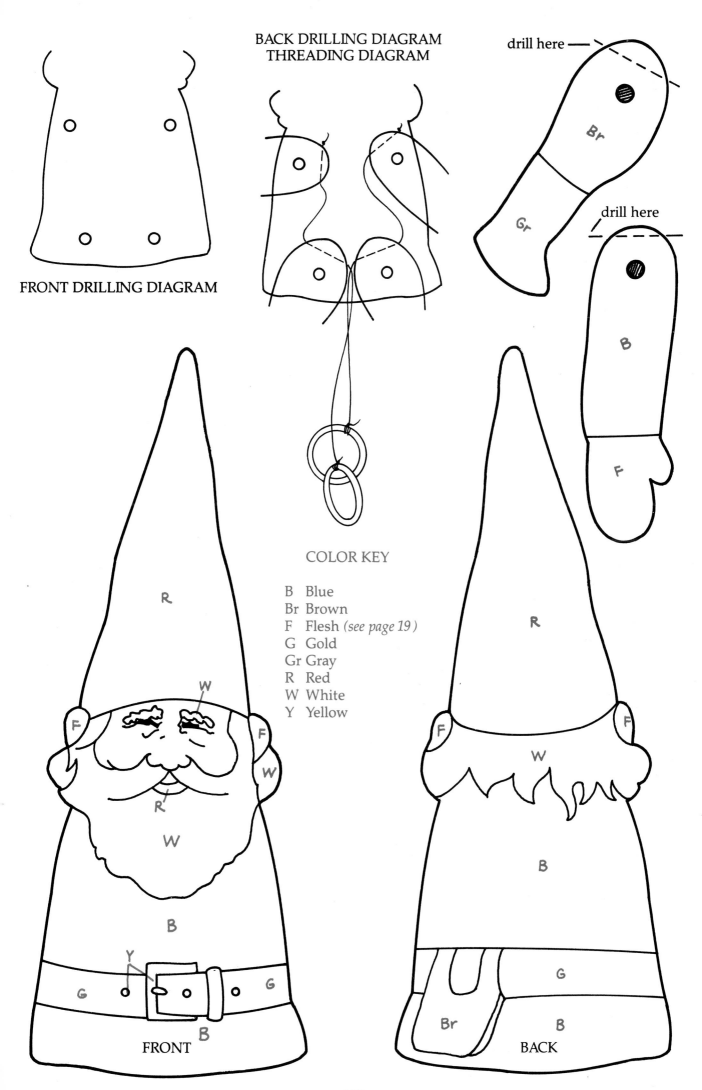

FRONT DRILLING DIAGRAM

BACK DRILLING DIAGRAM
THREADING DIAGRAM

drill here

drill here

COLOR KEY

B Blue
Br Brown
F Flesh (*see page 19*)
G Gold
Gr Gray
R Red
W White
Y Yellow

FRONT

BACK

107

"Baby's Sleeping" Pillow

Note: Before beginning, read General Directions for Painting on Fabric on page 20.

SKILL LEVEL: Intermediate

MATERIALS: Red polka dot cotton fabric, two 11 x 10" pieces. Medium-weight red cord, ⅓ yard. Novelty piping: red polka dot, ⅝ yard; white with red print, 1⅛ yards. Ruffled eyelet trim, ½" wide, ⅝ yard. White pearl cotton. Fiberfill. Matching thread. Muslin. Graphite paper.

Acrylic paint: red, green, blue, yellow, pink, gray, white, brown. Fine paintbrush. Rapidograph pen.

DIRECTIONS: Trace and use pattern to cut two circles from muslin; set one aside for backing. Transfer design to center of circle using graphite paper. Paint design following photograph for colors. Let dry, then outline painted areas with rapidograph pen.

With raw edges even, sew red polka dot piping to right side of painted circle. To end piping, cut out about ½" of inner cord at one end, turn edges of empty fabric tube to inside, and insert opposite end into empty fabric tube. With raw edges even, sew ruffled eyelet trim to circle over piping. Sew backing to painted circle with right sides facing, raw edges even, and trims in between, leaving opening for turning. Turn to right side and slip-stitch opening closed.

Center painted circle on right side of red polka dot fabric, with short edges at top and bottom; slip-stitch in place, leaving ruffled eyelet free. Trace and transfer "shhhh" above circle, and "baby's sleeping" below circle using graphite paper. Hand-embroider words in outline

shhhh

baby's sleeping

stitch using white pearl cotton (see Embroidery Stitch Details, page 18). With raw edges even, sew white/red piping around edges of pillow front. Sew ends of red cord to front top edge of pillow with raw edges even, about ½" in from each corner.

Sew red polka dot fabrics together with right sides facing and raw edges even, leaving opening for turning. Turn to right side; stuff with fiberfill until plump. Fold raw edges at opening to inside, and slip-stitch opening closed. Hang pil-

low around doorknob when your little gnome is asleep!

ADAPTATION: Embroider a message of your choice.

Gnomelife Quilt

Note: Before beginning, read General Directions for Sewing on page 17; for Appliqué on page 17; for Painting on Fabric on page 20; and for Embroidery on page 18.

SKILL LEVEL: Advanced

MATERIALS: Cotton or cotton-blend fabric, 45″ wide: follow *Color Key* for colors and yardages (in parentheses); for colors with no yardage amount, ⅛ yard or less is needed. Thread to match all fabrics. Acrylic paint: red, white, yellow, pink. Brown waterproof fine line marking pen. Rapidograph pen. Embroidery floss: black, brown, gold, lavender. White 4-ply orlon yarn. Batting, 75″ square. Extra-wide double-fold bias seam tape, 9 yards white. Tracing paper. Pencil. Tailor's chalk. Yardstick. Tape measure.

DIRECTIONS: Follow *Cutting Key* to cut all pieces necessary for constructing quilt top, backing, and border appliqué pieces; all measurements include ¼″ seam allowance. Trace separate actual-size patterns for each appliqué piece from *Foldout B* and use to cut out appliqué pieces from designated fabrics following *Color Key,* and adding ¼″ seam allowance (follow individual directions for Block 5; use patterns for Block 1 in reverse for Block 9).

Paint all face and hand pieces and let dry before starting to appliqué; paint faces and hands flesh, blending in pink for cheeks. Draw all eyes, noses, and mouths with brown marking pen.

Appliquéd Blocks: Transfer major outlines of each design to center of background squares: Blocks 2, 4, 6, and 8 are worked on yellow-gold background squares; all other blocks are worked on royal blue background squares. Machine-appliqué pieces to background squares following patterns; refer to individual directions for each block for details.

Block 1: Machine-embroider fine lines on bird with white thread using zigzag satin stitch.

Block 2: For flap on boy's

pants, fold bottom edge only to wrong side and hand-appliqué in place; machine-appliqué sides and top edge. Machine-embroider fine lines on boy's shirt and girl's dress with matching thread using zigzag satin stitch. Outline-stitch strings on hanging hearts with three strands of black embroidery floss in needle.

Block 3: Machine-appliqué brown strips and yellow windows over polka dot background pieces. For windowpane effect, machine-embroider pane lines with brown thread using zigzag satin stitch. Machine-embroider window on church steeple with orange thread using zigzag satin stitch.

Block 4: Machine-embroider red lines on kerchief and skirt, green line on vest, beige lines on basket and mouse, white lines on candle, and brown tree trunk using zigzag satin stitch. Outline-stitch flower on vest with two strands of lavender floss in needle; outline-stitch string on hanging heart with three strands of black embroidery floss in needle.

Block 5: Cut entire tree shape from hunter green fabric; appliqué to background square first. Cut out all other pieces following *Color Key.* Appliqué pieces to background tree, overlapping layers from dark to light colors, ending with white "snow" as top layer.

Block 6: Outline nose and eyelids with rapidograph pen. Work eyebrows in long and short stitch using three strands of white embroidery floss in needle. Work seeds in French knots using two strands each of gold and brown embroidery floss in needle. Machine-embroider all fine lines with matching thread using zigzag satin stitch.

Block 7: Work as for Block 3, omitting reference to church.

Block 8: Outline father's eyelid with rapidograph pen. Work eyebrows in long and short stitch using three strands of white embroidery floss in nee-

dle. Machine-embroider fine lines on mother's kerchief and sleeves with maroon thread; work all other fine lines with matching thread.

Block 9: Work same as for Block 1; design will be exact reverse.

Quilt Assembly: Separate framing strips into horizontal and vertical piles by color. Machine-appliqué red hearts to white framing strips and white hearts to red framing strips as follows: Pin four hearts on each short strip, and six hearts on each long strip *(see photograph for placement).* Machine-appliqué hearts to strips using matching thread.

Following *Assembly Diagram,* sew red vertical framing strips to side edges of Blocks 2, 4, 6, and 8, then sew red horizontal framing strips to top and bottom edges of these blocks (make sure all hearts face in same direction as design). Sew white horizontal framing strips to top and bottom edges of Blocks 1, 3, 5, 7, and 9, then sew white vertical strips to side edges of these blocks. Join Blocks 1, 4, and 7 together vertically with blue horizontal divider strips as shown; also sew blue divider strips to edges at top and bottom. Repeat for Blocks 2, 5, 8 and 3, 6, 9 in same manner. Connect sections with blue vertical divider strips, also sewing strips to outer side edges.

Sew white horizontal border strips to top and bottom edges of pieced center, then sew white vertical border strips to side edges. Appliqué large red hearts and small trees on blue outer strips following *Assembly Diagram.* Appliqué large tree to each corner square as shown. Sew one strip to each side of quilt so hearts and trees face outward. Sew corner squares to both ends of top and bottom strips following diagram; sew strips in place.

Sew backing pieces together, making one 75½" square; press seam. Arrange backing, wrong side up, on large flat surface.

Center layer of batting over backing; trim if necessary. Position quilt top, right side up, over batting. Pin layers together horizontally, vertically, and diagonally using large safety pins. Baste layers together near raw edges. Sandwich raw outer edges of quilt and backing with double-fold bias seam tape; slip-stitch tape to quilt top, then to backing, overlapping ends.

TUFTING DIAGRAM

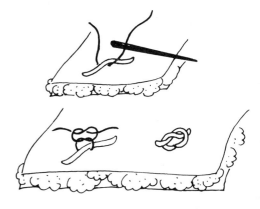

ALTERNATE TUFTING DIAGRAM

Following *Tufting Diagram,* or *Alternate Tufting Diagram,* use orlon yarn to tuft quilt at: corners of each appliquéd block; small corner hearts on each frame; evenly spaced along blue divider strips and white border strips; in center of each heart and tree on outer strips and corners. Remove all pins and basting.

ADAPTATIONS: Each block can be used as pillow front, placemat, or, when collected together, as a child's soft book. You may want to use batting and backing and quilt around designs for a three-dimensional effect. Stop at blue border and use as tablecloth. Make table runner or mantel skirt using outside borders.

See following page for Cutting Key *and* Foldout B *for* Color Key

111

ASSEMBLY DIAGRAM

CUTTING KEY FOR QUILT

ROYAL BLUE FABRIC

4	corner squares	6½ x 6½"
4	outer strips	64 x 6½"
12	horizontal divider strips	17½ x 2"
4	vertical divider strips	57½ x 2"
5	background squares	11½ x 11½"

WHITE FABRIC

2	backing pieces	38 x 75½"
2	horizontal border strips	57½ x 3¾"
2	vertical border strips	64 x 3¾"
10	horizontal framing strips	11½ x 3½"
10	vertical framing strips	17½ x 3½"
80	small hearts	
4	large tree tops	
24	small tree tops	

RED FABRIC

8	vertical framing strips	11½ x 3½"
8	horizontal framing strips	17½ x 3½"
100	small hearts	
28	large hearts	

YELLOW-GOLD FABRIC

4	background squares	11½ x 11½"

KELLY GREEN FABRIC

4	bottom branches for large tree
24	bottom branches for small tree

HUNTER GREEN FABRIC

24	middle branches for small tree

GREEN GINGHAM FABRIC

4	middle branches for large tree

Puppet Family in a Cupboard

Note: Before beginning, read General Directions for Painting on Fabric on page 20 and for Appliqué on page 17.

SKILL LEVEL: Advanced

MATERIALS: Muslin, 45" wide, 2 yards. Large scraps felt: red, blue, white, yellow, gold, gray, purple, chartreuse, pink. Gingham, 45" wide, ½ yard each: red, light green. Cotton fabric, 45" wide, 1 yard each: hunter green, red, yellow-gold; ½ yard each: white, kelly green. Yellow yarn. Grosgrain ribbon, ⅜" wide, 3⅓ yards chartreuse; 3 yards red. Batting. Thread to match fabrics. Graphite paper. Acrylic paint: red, yellow, white, blue, pink, gray. Brown waterproof fine line marking pen. Rapidograph pen.

DIRECTIONS: *Puppets:* Enlarge and trace main outline of each puppet pattern and transfer to muslin using graphite paper. Trace separate patterns for each pattern to cut appliqué from main design. Following photograph for colors, use each pattern to cut one appliqué piece from felt; cut two pieces for beard.

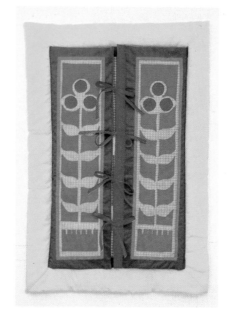

Paint face and hands flesh (*see page 19*); and then transfer face markings to muslin using graphite paper. Paint cheeks pink, shading gradually. For children, paint white eyes and blue irises; paint mouths pink. Draw in eyebrows and facial features with brown marking pen; for adults, highlight features and fill in eyes with rapidograph pen.

For father, sew beard pieces together around edges, then baste moustache to beard, matching top edges and overlapping ends of mouth. Topstitch around moustache and mouth. For girl's hair, braid yellow yarn into two braids, each about 3" long; attach to girl's head between placement marks, just below her hairline. Topstitch all appliqué pieces to muslin, sewing ⅛" away from edge of felt without turning under raw edges.

Cut out puppet pieces along marked outlines. With right sides facing and raw edges even, sew puppet fronts to backs, leaving bottom edges open; be careful not to catch father's beard in seamline. Turn puppets to right side and set aside.

Wall Hanging: Cut one 23½ x 14½" background and two 6 x 14½" pockets from red gingham. Cut two 5½ x 14½" pocket cuffs from white fabric. Press long edges of cuffs ¼" to wrong side, then press cuff in half lengthwise with raw edges inside. Sandwich one long edge of each pocket between pressed edges of cuff and topstitch in place. Press cuffs over to right side of gingham pockets; baste along side edges to secure. Pin one pocket to background, flush with bottom edges. Press lower edge of remaining pocket ¼" to wrong side; pin turned edge to background 8½" above bottom of background. Sew pockets to background along sides and bottom edges.

Cut two 22 x 31" pieces from muslin for backing, and one 21½ x 30½" piece from batting. Cen-

ter and baste batting between muslin pieces with muslin edges even. Center red gingham piece over muslin; sew to muslin along each side, ¼" from raw edges. Cut two 23½ x 1½" and two 16½ x 2" strips from hunter green fabric. Pin 23½" strips to each long edge of gingham center with right sides facing and raw edges even; sew to gingham and muslin backing. Fold green strips over to right side and press lightly in place. Topstitch close to seamline. Sew 16½" strips to top and bottom of gingham center in same manner; topstitch close to seam. For yellow-gold border, cut two pieces 31 x 3¼" and two pieces 22 x 2¾" from yellow-gold fabric. Center and pin 31" strips to side green strips with right sides facing and raw edges even. Sew in place, starting at lower corner of green strip and ending at upper corner, leaving 2½" unsewn at top and bottom; repeat for opposite side. Center, pin, and sew short strips to top and bottom green strips, leaving 3" unsewn at left and right edges. Fold strips to right side, matching edges of muslin. Miter raw edges at corners, trim, and sew together. Fold raw outer edges of muslin and yellow-gold strips ½" to inside; slip-stitch edges together.

For doors, cut two 8 x 26½" pieces from hunter green fabric; cut one 1½ x 26½" right front strip, one 9 x 26½" right lining, and one 8 x 26½" left lining from red fabric. Cut two 5 x 22½" "windows" from green gingham. Transfer appliqué design to center of each gingham window using graphite paper. Cut two each of the appliqué pieces from kelly green and red fabrics following photograph. Pin in marked position on windows, then machine-appliqué using zigzag satin stitch. Center one window over each hunter green door; baste in place. Cover raw edges of window with chartreuse grosgrain ribbon and sew in place ¹⁄₁₆" from all edges, overlapping ends. Sew red strip to

left edge of one hunter green door with raw edges even; this will become righthand door. Cut red grosgrain ribbon into eight 12" lengths. With raw edges even, sew ribbons to long edges of each door, spaced 5½" apart (sew ribbons to red strip for right door, and to green right edge for left door). Sew red backing pieces to doors with right sides facing, raw edges even, and ribbons in between; leave opening in each for turning. Turn to right side, exposing ribbons; slip-stitch openings closed. Position right and left doors directly over large background piece. Topstitch outer edges of doors directly over edges of green strips on background. Remove all basting. Make loops from scraps of fabric, and slip-stitch loops to back of hanging. Insert dowel or curtain rod through loops and hang. Insert puppets into pockets.

ADAPTATION: Make puppets from terry cloth, embroider features, and use as washcloths.

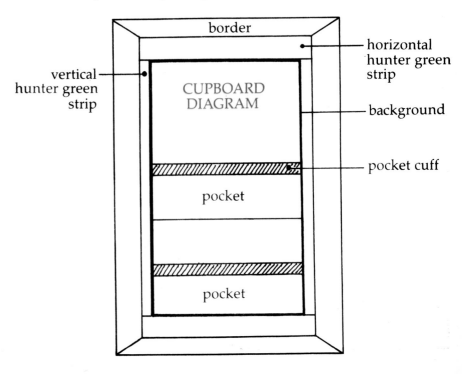

CUPBOARD DIAGRAM

border

horizontal hunter green strip

vertical hunter green strip

background

pocket cuff

pocket

pocket

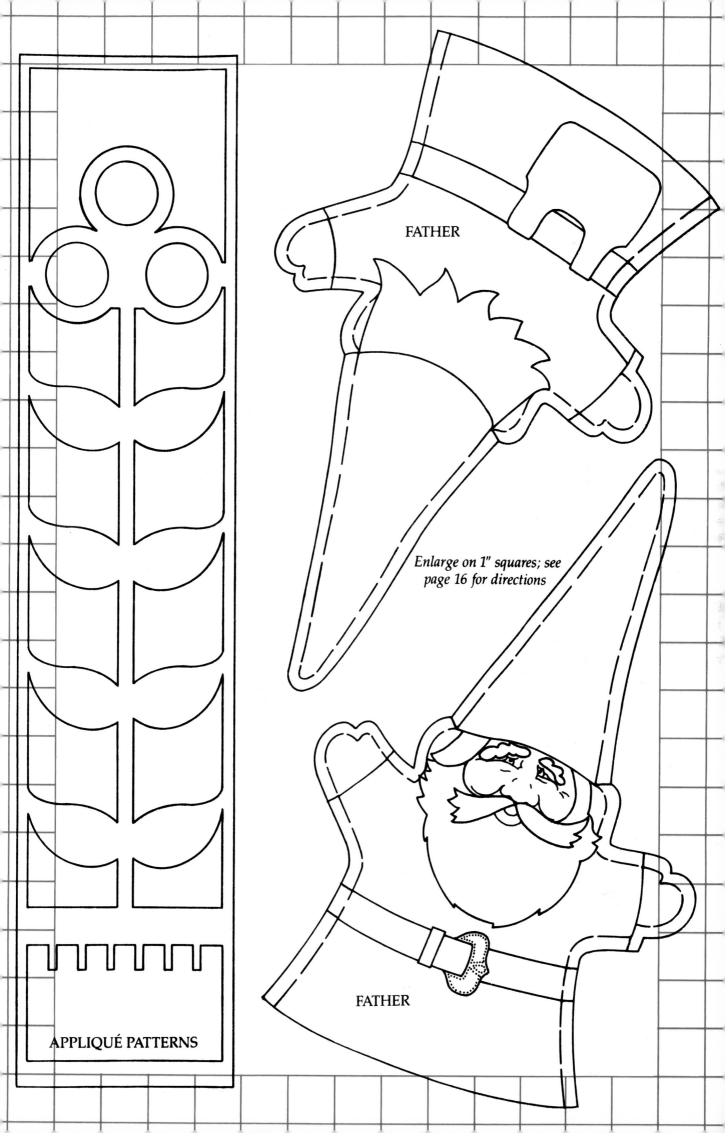

FATHER

*Enlarge on 1" squares; see
page 16 for directions*

FATHER

APPLIQUÉ PATTERNS

MOTHER

BOY

BOY

Enlarge on 1" squares; see page 16 for directions

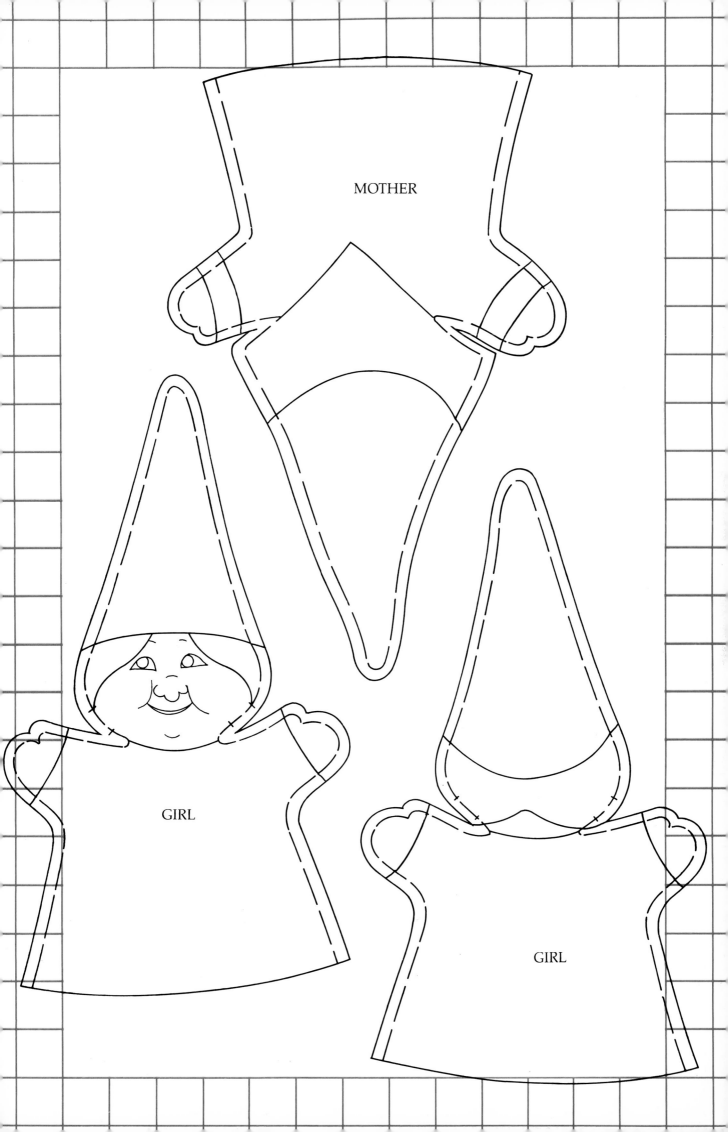

MOTHER

GIRL

GIRL

Christmas Day

There is a family understanding that gifts cannot be opened until John and I are up; but no one has told the children not to go downstairs. In the half light of dawn we hear them whispering, then sneaking quietly past our door. We follow shortly, not wanting to miss the joy in their faces when they see the tree.

At last it is time. The stockings are taken down. The hands plunge in, until they are elbow deep, searching for the best surprise at the toe, and for the shiny new penny that is always there.

After the children have opened all their gifts, they offer us ours. We ask only that they have made the gifts themselves. Genevieve has made a straw wreath and Rodney a dust broom. Gabrielle opens her present to us herself. It is a Christmas card envelope with jagged cuts around the edges and a ribbon at one corner. An ornament, she says, and together we hang it on the tree....

Simple Stocking

Note: Before beginning, read General Directions for Appliqué on page 17.

SKILL LEVEL: Elementary

MATERIALS: Cotton fabric, 45" wide: red polka dot, ½ yard; white, ½ yard for lining; white with red print, about ¼ yard. Wax crayons: red, orange, flesh, pink, blue, brown, yellow, gray. White ½" rickrack, 1¼ yards. White thread. Batting. Cord for hanging. Graphite paper. Paper towels.

DIRECTIONS: Trace appliqué pattern, including outline, and transfer outline and design to white fabric using graphite paper. Using wax crayons, color face and ears flesh; blend in pink on cheeks and tips of ears. Color cap red with orange highlights. Color mouth red. Color shirt pale blue, belt and pants brown, buckle yellow, and boots gray. Sandwich colored gnome between layers of paper towels. Press with dry iron to remove wax from design; change towels often until wax is removed. Cut out gnome, adding ¼" seam allowance around edges.

Enlarge and trace pattern for stocking as indicated (dot/dash line is for placement of gnome only). Use pattern to cut two pieces each from red polka dot fabric and white lining fabric, reversing pattern to cut second pieces. Enlarge letters from alphabet on page 124 if desired and use to trace name; use letter patterns to cut out letters from white fabric with red print, adding ¼" seam allowance around edges. Arrange letters as desired on stocking and machine-appliqué in place. Machine-appliqué gnome to stocking where indicated. Baste white rickrack, centered over seamline, all around front of stocking. Baste batting to wrong side of each red polka dot stocking piece; sew red polka dot pieces together with right sides facing, raw edges even, and rickrack in between. Remove basting. Turn stocking to right side. Sew lining pieces together with raw edges even, leaving top open; do not turn. Cut two 6 x 9¼" cuffs from white fabric. Sew short edges of cuffs together, making circle of fabric. Press one long edge ¼" to wrong side. Cut batting to fit cuff; trim away ¼" along raw edges and baste to wrong side of cuff. With right sides facing and raw edges even, sew cuff to top of lining, matching side seams. Insert lining into stocking. Fold cuff over to right side of stocking so pressed edge covers raw edge; slip-stitch in place, easing as necessary. Slip-stitch ends of cord inside cuff to make a loop for hanging.

ADAPTATION: Have child draw and color design of his/her choice for appliqué.

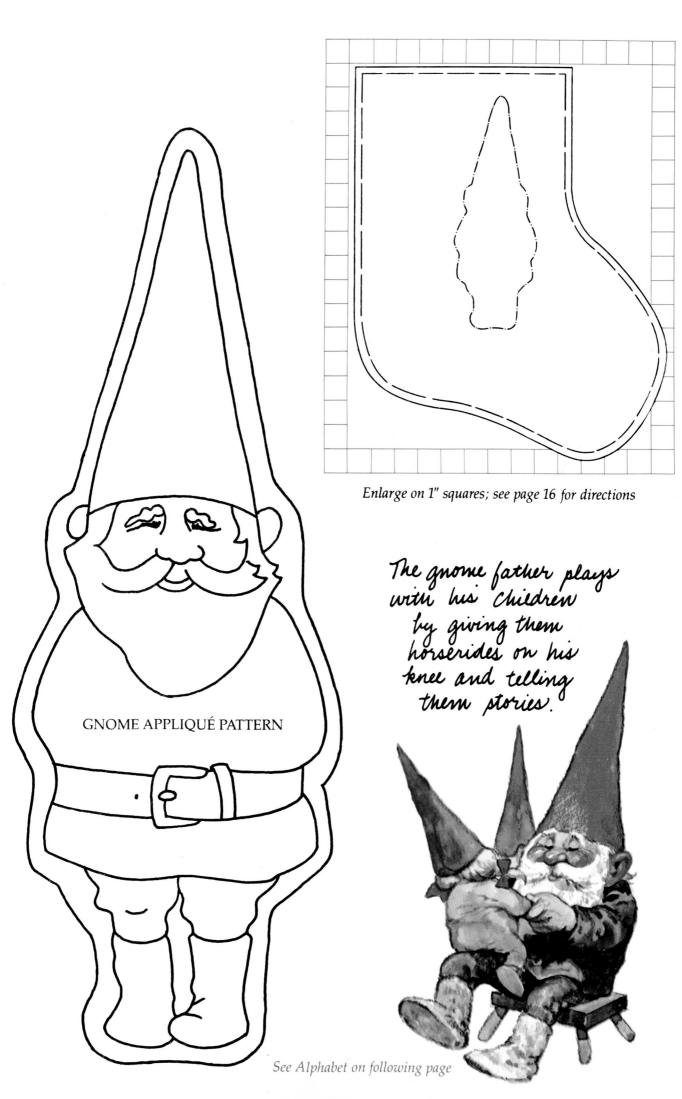

GNOME APPLIQUÉ PATTERN

Enlarge on 1" squares; see page 16 for directions

The gnome father plays with his children by giving them horserides on his knee and telling them stories.

See Alphabet on following page

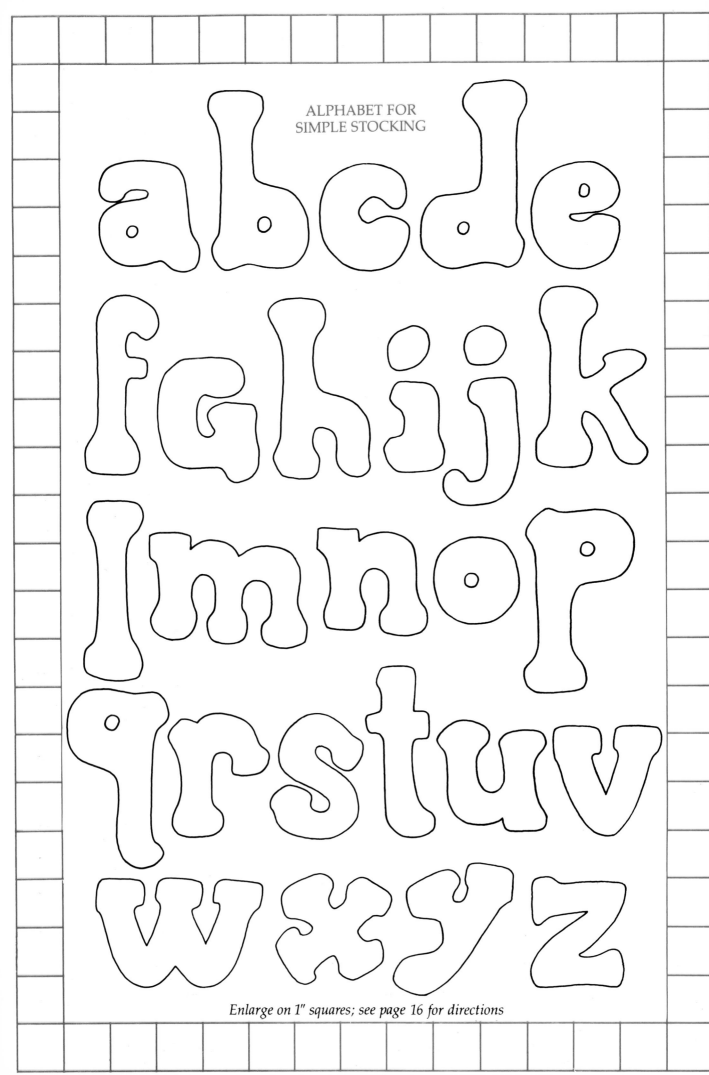

ALPHABET FOR
SIMPLE STOCKING

a b c d e
f g h i j k
l m n o p
q r s t u v
w x y z

Enlarge on 1" squares; see page 16 for directions

Holidaytime Stocking

Note: Before beginning, read General Directions for Painting on Fabric on page 20 and for Appliqué on page 17.

SKILL LEVEL: Intermediate

MATERIALS: Muslin, 45" wide, ¼ yard. Acrylic paint: colors listed in *Color Key*. Fine paintbrushes. Graphite paper. Rapidograph pen. Green calico, ½ yard for backing; scraps of 8 different calicos in shades of green. Green gingham, ¼ yard. White cotton, 36" wide, 1 yard for lining. Batting. Green cord, 6".

DIRECTIONS: Enlarge and trace separate patterns for outline of stocking and for each patchwork piece; add ¼" seam allowance around all edges of each piece. Use patchwork patterns 1 and 4 to cut pieces from green gingham; cut all other patchwork pieces from assorted calico fabrics. Use stocking outline in reverse to cut backing; also cut two lining pieces. Sew patchwork pieces together with right sides facing and raw edges even following pattern.

Trace actual-size painting patterns on following pages, including outlines. Transfer each outline and design (but not placement numbers) to muslin using graphite paper. Following *Color Key* and directions below, paint each design. Numbers on patterns indicate very light (1), light (2), or dark (3) shades of same color; for letters with no numbers, paint section in a medium shade.

Paint all faces and hands flesh; blend in pink for cheeks with touches of red. For each adult male gnome, paint white hair and beard, red cap highlighted with orange, blue shirt, brown pants, and medium gray boots. Paint young male gnomes in same way but with yellow hair. For each adult female gnome, paint white hair, dark gray cap highlighted with medium gray, medium gray kerchief and blouse with maroon trim and cuffs, white apron, and grass green skirt (shaded to simulate folds). For Design 2, follow *Color Key* for clothes; paint each young female gnome with yellow hair, light grass green cap highlighted with dark shading, and a dark pink dress and bows. For Design 3, follow *Color Key* for clothes.

Paint all other areas of designs as indicated. For additional directions, read individual directions below. After all painting is completed, outline painted areas with rapidograph pen unless otherwise directed.

Design 1: Paint trunk and all branches of tree medium to light brown as desired. Paint tree in very light, light, and medium shades of grass green, making interior branches darker than exterior branches. Bottoms of boots should not be outlined with rapidograph.

Design 2: Paint entire stove very light yellow; paint interior of oven very light to medium brown. Shade tops of pies with medium and very light brown. Do not outline painted designs on stove or trim on apron. For a realistic touch, stroke very light gray wisps of steam above pies.

Design 3: Paint as directed following *Color Key*.

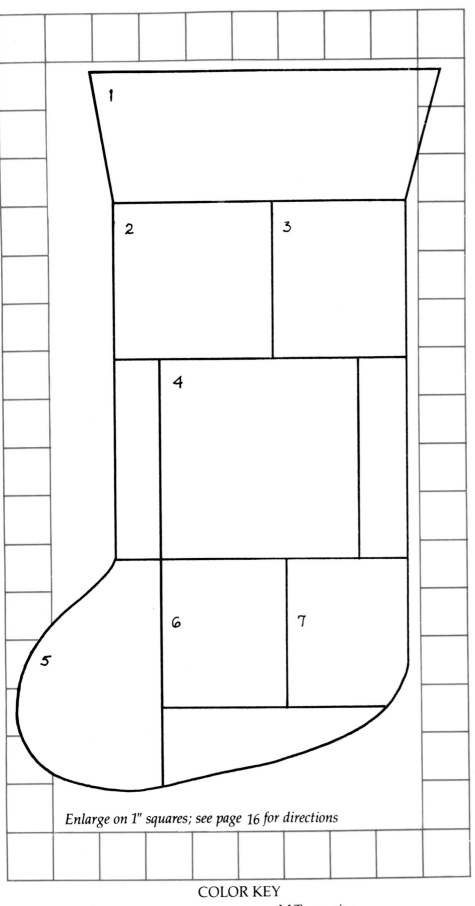

Enlarge on 1" squares; see page 16 for directions

COLOR KEY

A White	M Turquoise
B Flesh *(see page 19)*	N Brown
C Pink	O Gray
D Red ⎤ F	P Maroon
E Orange ⎦	
G Yellow ⎤ H	1 Very light
J Lime green	2 Light
K Grass green	Medium (no number)
L Blue	3 Dark

Design 4: Paint all shaded areas of tree dark grass green; paint unshaded areas light green. Paint stove very light yellow; shade interior of oven with very light gray and maroon; shade gray at top. Paint fruit pink with red highlights. Do not outline red ribbons held by birds or designs on stove.

Design 5: Shade as desired; use your imagination to achieve a natural effect.

Design 6: Paint pillows and border of coverlet white, then paint border designs. Paint figures inside dream cloud with very light shades of paint as indicated; highlight cloud with white and blue. Do not outline checks on coverlet or border designs.

Design 7: Shade mouse with yellow and orange. Do not outline trim on inset of door. Write male's name on tag attached to hanging cap.

Hand-appliqué painted muslin pieces to center of patchwork pieces following placement numbers. Cut two pieces of batting to fit stocking. Baste batting to wrong sides of patchwork front and calico backing. Sew front to backing leaving top open; clip curves and turn to right side. Sew lining pieces together leaving top open; do not turn to right side. Cut two 3 x 15½" cuffs from green gingham. Sew short ends of cuffs together, making circle of fabric. Press one long edge ¼" to wrong side. Cut batting to fit cuff; trim away ¼" along raw edges and baste to wrong side of cuff. With right sides facing and raw edges even, sew cuff to top of lining, matching side seams. Insert lining into stocking. Fold cuff over to right side of stocking so. pressed edge covers raw edge; slip-stitch in place, easing as necessary. Slip-stitch ends of green cord inside cuff to make loop for hanging.

ADAPTATIONS: Use painted motifs to decorate cloth items of your choice. Embroider all painted areas.

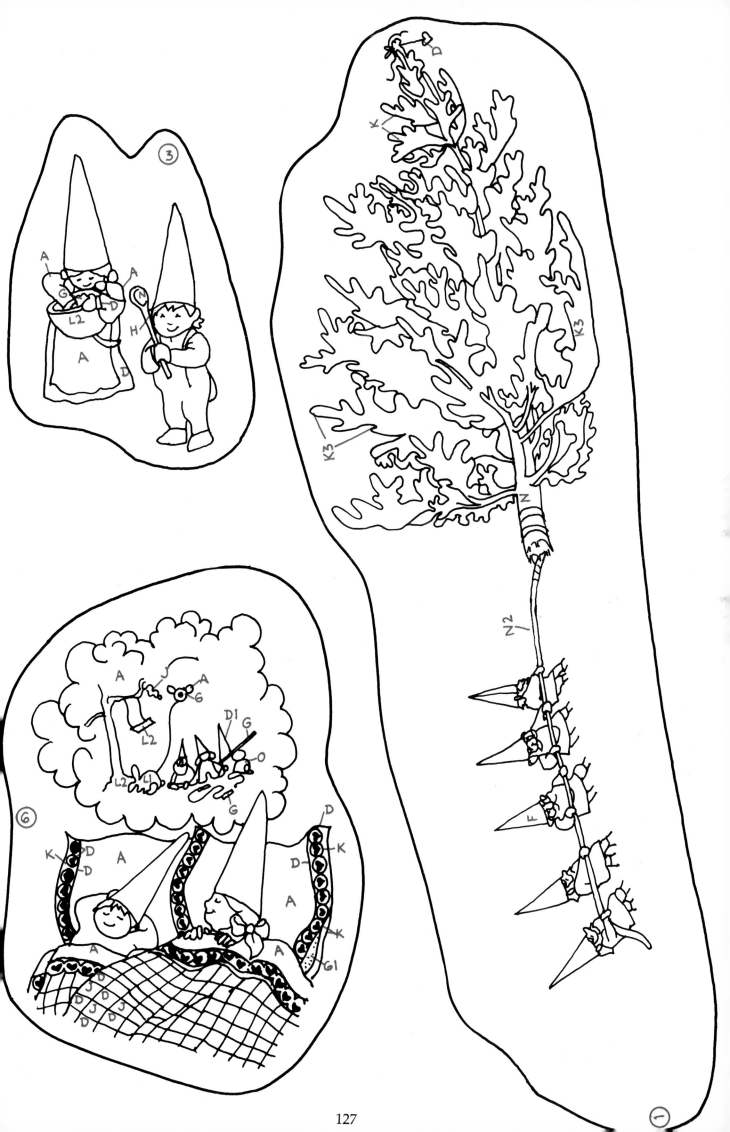

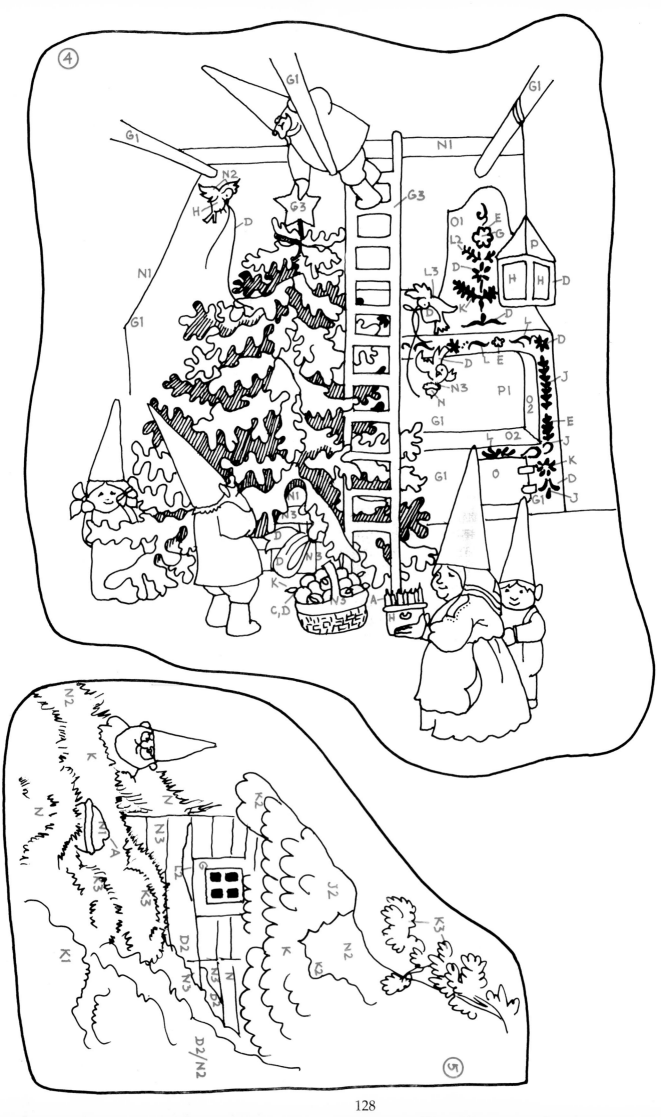

Candlelight Festival Stocking

Note: Before beginning, read General Directions for Embroidery on page 18. See Foldout A *for Color and* Stitch Keys

SKILL LEVEL: Advanced. Knowledge of embroidery necessary.

MATERIALS: Cotton fabric, 45" wide, ½ yard each: red polka dot, medium-weight white, lightweight white for lining; ¼ yard white with red strawberry print. Batting. Six-strand embroidery floss, one skein of each color listed in *Color Key* unless otherwise indicated in parentheses. White thread. Graphite paper. Embroidery hoop. Embroidery needles.

DIRECTIONS: Trace actual-size pattern, including stocking outline, from *Foldout A*. Cut 22 x 16" piece from medium-weight white fabric. Center pattern over right side of fabric, leaving equal margins around all edges; transfer embroidery design to fabric using graphite paper.

Embroider stocking following *Color* and *Stitch Keys*, using three strands floss in needle unless otherwise directed. Work pine boughs around perimeter

Key, then work gold metallic halos around flames. Finally, embroider all little details around perimeter of stocking following *Color* and *Stitch Keys*.

When embroidery is completed, steam-press gently on padded surface, with embroidered surface face down. Carefully trim edges of fabric, leaving ½" seam allowance around stocking outline. Sew around stocking following outline. Fold raw edges to wrong side along outline, clipping curves where necessary; press carefully.

Enlarge and trace pattern for background stocking from *Foldout A* and use to cut two red polka dot stockings and two white linings, reversing pattern to cut second pieces. Center embroidery on right side of one red polka dot stocking; pin, then slip-stitch to secure. Cut two pieces of batting, ¼" smaller than polka dot stocking pieces. Baste batting to wrong side of each piece. Sew polka dot stocking pieces together, leaving top open. Clip curves and turn to right side. Sew lining pieces together, leaving top open; do not turn to right side.

Cut two 7 x 13½" cuffs from white fabric with strawberry print. Sew short edges of cuffs together, making a circle of fabric. Press one long edge ¼" to wrong side. Cut batting to fit cuff; trim away ¼" along raw edges and baste to wrong side of cuff. With right sides facing and raw edges even, sew cuff to top of lining, matching side seams. Insert lining into stocking. Fold cuff over to right side of stocking, so pressed edge covers raw edge; slip-stitch in place, easing as necessary. Make a loop for hanging from white fabric; slip-stitch inside cuff.

ADAPTATION: Isolate any of the embroidery designs and use as motif for apron, mantel skirt, or napkins.

of design first: straight-stitch needles on all finely drawn boughs with ice green floss, and highlight by straight-stitching over with chartreuse; for boughs drawn with heavy lines, outline-stitch branches with russet brown, then straight-stitch pine needles using hunter green floss. Work ribbon in red split stitch with brick red outline. Work center tree entirely in straight stitch, layering colors: work first layer with ice green and chartreuse, highlighting branches at random, then work grass green around and over first stitches. Embroider all candles in same way following *Tree Candle Diagram*. Finally, work forest and hunter green branches over first branches and around candles.

Work star at top of tree in gold metallic satin stitch (*see Star Diagram*). Embroider gnomes fol-

lowing *Color Key*; for females' vests, work French knots and highlight with bright colors as desired. Female gnomes' skirts have shadows of forest and grass green along folds. Outline male gnomes' shirts with royal blue. When combining colors for special effects (*Color Key #*s 7, 12, 22, 24, 33, 35), such as shading on caps, embroider with two strands of dark color and one strand of light color in needle. When gnomes are complete, embroider angels and stars following *Color Key*; fill in top angel's hair with French knots. Work flowers at top in French knots, using two strands of carnation and two strands of rose in needle for a special raised effect. Work candles at top in white split stitch; outline-stitch drips with ivory floss, making French knots at ends. Work all flames following *Color*

Pine Cone Wreath and Gnome Procession

Note: Before beginning, read General Directions for Woodworking on page 16 for additional materials and directions.

SKILL LEVEL: Intermediate. Some knowledge of woodworking useful.

MATERIALS: *For Wreath*: Large plastic foam ring. Medium and large pine cones. Dry pods as desired. Thirty small white dried flowers. Stiff brush. Shallow baking pan. Plastic or aluminum screen. Wire cutters. #18 gauge floral wire. Florist's picks. *For Figures*: Mahogany, ½" thick. Sloyd knife. Artists' oil colors: colors listed in *Color Key*. Fine and medium paintbrushes. Varnish. Wood glue. ¾" wire nails. Strand of thirty miniature white lights.

DIRECTIONS: *Wreath*: Prepare cones as follows: Wash all cones in water. Using stiff brush, remove any dirt that has hardened on scales. (Some cones will be covered with sticky pitch, which must be removed as follows: Line a shallow pan with aluminum foil and place cones in it; bake in a 200° F. oven until pitch melts. Remove cones from oven and let cool, then rinse thoroughly with water. Prop up plastic or aluminum screen in warm, dry place so air can circulate above and below it, then place cones on screen, leaving space between them to allow for expansion. Let dry for about two weeks or until cones are fully expanded with stiff scales.) Wire each cone following *Wiring Diagram*; twist wire ends together as shown. Wire three or four cones to each florist's pick. Insert picks into plastic foam ring until entire ring is covered on top and side edges. Add pods and flowers.

Figures: For a full procession, carve three large adult males and females, two large girls and boys. For wreath, carve one small adult male and female, one small girl and boy, one backview male and female, and one house. Measure the length and width of the piece you wish to carve and cut an appropriate-size piece from mahogany. Transfer pattern to wood. Whittle away excess wood around design using Sloyd knife. Continue lines drawn on front along side edges; for pieces that are carved on both sides (the two large adults and the two large children), transfer design to other side of wood same as for front. Carefully whittle wood along drawn lines to round edges and bring out features and details. Pieces that will be placed on wreath do not need to be carved on both sides. To carve slot for holding lights, follow *Hand Diagram* above large boy gnome and whittle away space between the hands; do this carefully because pieces are fragile. From mahogany, cut six 1 x 3 x ½" bases, and four 2 x 1 x ½" bases.

Paint figures following *Color Key*; paint bases green. Paint red design on woman's blouse after you paint blouse gray. Varnish as directed on page 16. Glue adult gnomes on 1 x 3 x ½" bases; glue large children on 2 x 1 x ½" bases. Nail bases to secure after glue dries.

Assembly: Arrange gnomes that are on bases on mantel as if they are walking toward wreath. Prop smaller gnomes on wreath at random, facing uncarved side toward wreath; glue lightly if necessary. String lights all over wreath and through gnomes' hands as shown in photograph.

ADAPTATION: Use wreath as table centerpiece; decorate with ribbon, baby's breath, and candles.

SMALL ADULT MALE

BACKVIEW ADULT MALE

HAND DIAGRAM

SMALL ADULT FEMALE

BACKVIEW ADULT FEMALE

LARGE BOY

LARGE GIRL

SMALL GIRL

SMALL BOY

WIRING DIAGRAM

HOUSE

LARGE ADULT FEMALE

LARGE ADULT MALE

COLOR KEY

R   Cadmium red medium
F   Flesh
Y   Cadmium yellow medium
P   Pink
G   Green
Gr   Gray
B   Ultramarine blue
Bl   Black
Br   Vandyke brown
W   White

Christmas breakfast is a hurried but festive affair. Because there is so much to do for Christmas dinner, we have planned simple food for this meal. Still, we fuss over decorating the table. A stenciled table runner covers the linen tablecloth from Finland, and everyone's place is specially marked with a candle placecard. There is homemade bread, cheese, fruit, nuts, and eggs. And although it is traditional in Scandinavia to hide an almond in one bowl of rice porridge, we prefer to place three almonds in each child's bowl of cereal. When they discover the almonds they are given an additional surprise.

After breakfast, the children return to play with their toys, while John and I set up for Christmas dinner. John will cook roast goose with prune and apple stuffing, red cabbage, and sugar brown potatoes. And of course there will be glogg, a hot spiced wine, to drink.

On my way upstairs to dress I pause a moment by the living room. The children are playing by the tree, and the fire has warmed the room, which is filled with the scents of pine and almond and chocolate. For me the feelings I have at this moment are the greatest gift of all.

Gnomeware

SKILL LEVEL: Advanced. Knowledge of throwing on the wheel necessary.

MATERIALS: Sharp instrument for trimming edges of shapes. Chamois cloth. Bowl of water. Calipers. Sponges. Kick-wheel or electric wheel for throwing. Gouge. #28 gauge bronze or copper wire stretched between two wooden handles. Reduction kiln. Cones: #s 8, 9, 10. Large bucket for glaze.

RECIPE FOR CLAY BODY
Fireclay . . . . 100 parts
Goldart 40
Redart 20
English Ball Clay 40
F4 4
Fine Grog 14

RECIPE FOR MATTE GLAZE (RUST, WHITE, BROWN)
Feldspar (Kingman) . . . 60 parts
Kaolin (Edgar Plastic
  Kaolin) 30
Flint 30
Dolomite 30

DIRECTIONS: Wedge clay thoroughly to remove air pockets. Throw clay onto revolving wheel and center it. Form bottoms, then form shapes as shown in diagrams. Use calipers to measure for uniform size.

Stamp for Teapot: Fashion stamp following diagrams and actual-size heart pattern; bisque-fire to cone #10 before making teapot.

Dinner Plates: 6 pounds of wet clay are needed; throw each plate to a wet diameter of 12¾".

Bowls: 3½ pounds of wet clay are needed; throw each bowl to a wet diameter of 6".

Tea Bowls: 1½ pounds of wet clay are needed; throw each bowl to a wet diameter of 4".

Egg Cups: 2½ pounds of wet clay are needed; throw off a hump. Throw six top halves to a wet diameter of 2"; throw six bottom halves to a wet diameter of 1½". Score rounded tops; attach tops to bottoms with slip.

Teapot: 10 pounds of wet clay are needed. Throw bowl; turn over and throw bottom. Incise holes for pouring in positions indicated by dash lines. Throw spout to 5" height; slice at a diagonal as shown in diagram. Score bowl around holes and edges of spout; attach spout to bowl using slip and smooth all edges. Flatten and pinch mouth of spout for easy pouring. For lid, throw bottom first, measuring to fit bowl; use gouge to make acute corner to fit. Turn lid over and throw rounded top with knob. Pull handle; score bowl and handle and attach handle

with slip. Stamp 7 hearts on each side of bowl from handle to spout using bisque-fired stamp; hold your hand inside pot as you stamp each heart. Also stamp base of handle where indicated by arrow.

Bisque-fire all pieces in a reduction kiln to cone #10. Let cool; apply glaze by pouring and dipping pieces. Fire glaze to cone #10.

BISQUE-FIRED
STAMP
(for decorating teapot)

See following page for additional diagrams

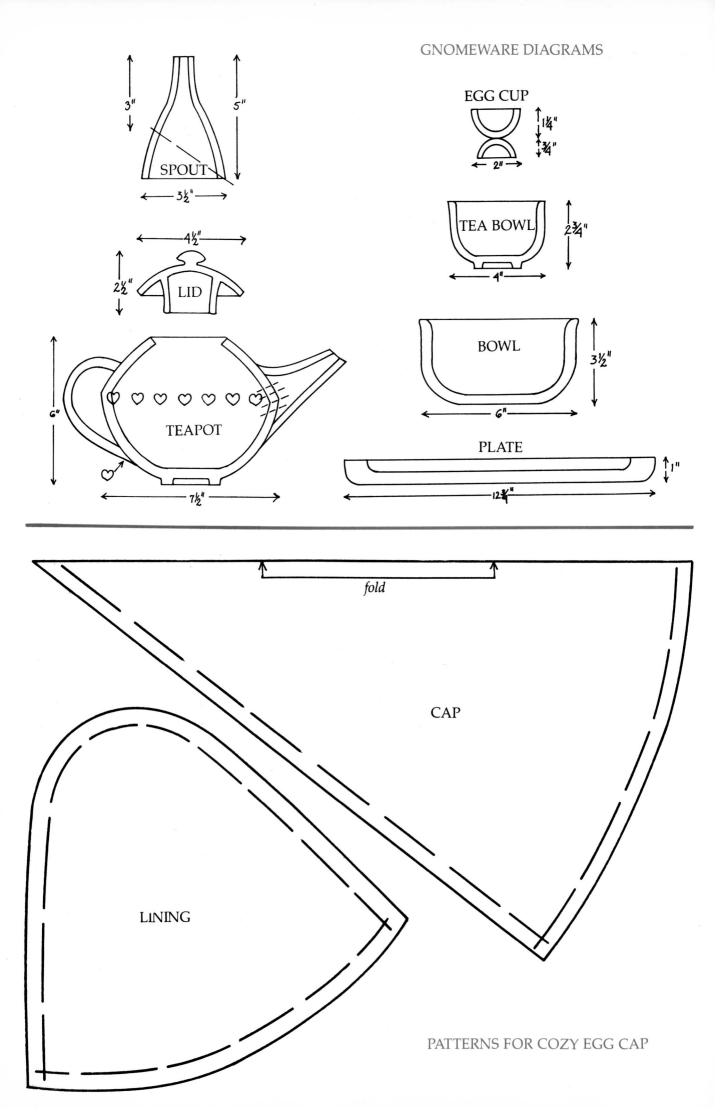

EGG CUP

1¼"

¾"

2"

TEA BOWL

2¾"

4"

SPOUT

3"

5"

3½"

BOWL

3½"

6"

4½"

2½"

LID

6"

TEAPOT

7½"

PLATE

1"

12¾"

fold

CAP

LINING

PATTERNS FOR COZY EGG CAP

Cozy Egg Cap

SKILL LEVEL: Elementary

MATERIALS: Large scrap red felt. Red cotton fabric for lining. Fiberfill. Red thread.

DIRECTIONS: Trace patterns and use to cut one cap from red felt and two lining pieces from red lining fabric. Sew seam on cap and turn cap to right side. Stuff top portion of cap with fiberfill. Sew lining pieces together with raw edges even. Insert lining into cap with wrong sides facing. Fold bottom edge of cap over lining and slip-stitch to lining. Cap will fit snugly over medium to large egg.

Heart Napkin Holders

SKILL LEVEL: Elementary

MATERIALS: ¼" basswood. Jig or coping saw. Sandpaper. Drill with ¼" bit. Green grosgrain ribbon, ¼" wide, ¼ yard for each. White acrylic paint. Medium paintbrush.

DIRECTIONS: Trace pattern and use to mark desired number of hearts on ¼" basswood. Cut out along marked lines with jig or coping saw. Sand edges until smooth. Drill two holes through each heart in positions indicated. Paint heart white; let dry. Thread grosgrain ribbon through holes; tie bow on one side, leaving loop large enough to hold napkin on other side.

ADAPTATIONS: Adapt color of paint to match table linen. Drill one centered hole and hang as ornament.

*Gnome working at the **Cap form** — a job that he hates!*

Placecard Holder

Note: Before beginning, read General Directions for Woodworking on page 16 for additional materials and directions.

SKILL LEVEL: Intermediate. Some knowledge of woodworking useful.

MATERIALS: Mahogany: 4½ x 2 x 1"; 1¼ x 1½ x ½" (base). Sloyd knife. Artists' oil colors: Cadmium red medium, Ultramarine blue, White, Black, Flesh, Vandyke brown, Gray, Green. Fine and medium paintbrushes. Varnish. Drill with ¼" bit. Wood glue. ¾" wire nail. Small candle, or ¼" dowel, 2" long.

DIRECTIONS: Using pattern transfer side view to each edge of 1" mahogany; transfer front view to each side, lining up top and bottom edges. Whittle away excess wood around design using Sloyd knife. Carve away front of gnome above and below arms following *Side View Diagram*; shaded area indicates section to be drilled. Redraw lines that have been carved away on front. Draw lines on back of piece to indicate edges of cap, hair, belt, shirt, and boots (continuing lines from front). Carefully whittle wood along drawn lines to round and bring out features and details (the piece will become fragile as more wood is whittled away). Drill hole into hands as indicated by shaded area. Make slot in base as shown in side view; this slot will later hold placecard. Sand base.

Paint figure and base, back and front, following photograph for color (paint belt yellow; pants brown; boots gray; if using dowel, paint to simulate candle). Varnish as directed on page 16. Glue gnome to base; secure with nail. Insert small candle or dowel into drilled hole. If candle is used, bend away from body to prevent scorching.

FRONT VIEW DIAGRAM   SIDE VIEW DIAGRAM

Stained Glass Decorations

SKILL LEVEL: Elementary. Knowledge of stained glass essential.

MATERIALS: Tracing paper. Construction paper. Scissors. Kerosene in small can. Masking tape. Glass cutter. Breaking pliers. Grozing pliers. ¼"-wide copper foil tape with adhesive backing. Burnisher. 60/40 solder. Soldering iron. Flux. Glass: types and colors listed in individual directions. ¾" wire nails. Needle-nosed wire cutters. #20 gauge wire for hanging. Liquid detergent. Bristle brush. Small paintbrush. Rags. Gray patina. Wood scrap large enough to accommodate designs. *See individual stained glass projects below and on following pages for additional materials.*

DIRECTIONS: Make two copies of pattern you are using—one for cutting (on tracing paper) and one for placement (on construction paper). Number each pattern piece, then cut out each piece from tracing paper only. Place one pattern piece at a time on glass, securing in place with tape underneath. Cut around pattern with glass cutter dipped in kerosene, alternately scoring and breaking away excess glass until entire piece has been cut out. For straight scores, snap glass apart with breaking pliers or by grasping glass firmly on each side of the score and bending down and outward, pressing evenly all the while. As you proceed, use grozing pliers to hone all cut edges so glass pieces fit pattern and align with one another.

Clean cut glass pieces to remove any dirt or oil. Copper foil all edges of each piece and burnish foil so it lies smooth and tight against glass.

Place construction paper pattern over wood piece. Position glass pieces on construction paper. Check fit. To maintain fit and hold glass in place, drive 8 to 10 wire nails around perimeter of design. With pieces in place, apply flux over all surfaces of foil. Further hold pieces together with small drops of solder. Solder all pieces together on one side. Let cool. Remove nails from wood; turn project over and solder reverse seams and outside edges.

Using liquid detergent and bristle brush, clean glass thoroughly. Apply gray patina to solder with paintbrush for pewter effect; wash again.

Male Gnome Sun Catcher: Cathedral glass: blue for suit; red for hat and mouth; gold for belt; brown for pants. Opalescent glass: gray for boots; beige for face and ears; white for hair, moustache, and beard *(see photograph).* Attach #20 gauge wire loop to base of cap at back for hanging.

Female Gnome Sun Catcher: Cathedral glass: red for vest and cuffs; green for skirt; dark gray for hat and shoes. Opalescent glass: white for sleeves and kerchief; light gray for hair; beige for face and hands *(see photograph).* Attach #20 gauge wire loop to base of cap at back.

Heart Sun Catcher: Red cathedral glass. Cut two heart halves from red glass. Make as directed. Attach #20 gauge wire loop to back of heart at center top for hanging.

Hanging Heart with Berries Sun Catcher: Cathedral glass: red for heart; green for leaves. Small red jewels for berries. #16 gauge wire for stems and branches.

Cut heart and leaves. Copper foil all pieces. Following *Hanging Heart Diagram,* cut wire for center stem and for two short and two long branches; bend branches as shown in diagram. Solder branches to center stem. Flux then solder all pieces, including jewels, to center stem and branches as shown in diagram. Attach #20 gauge wire loop near top of center branch at back for hanging.

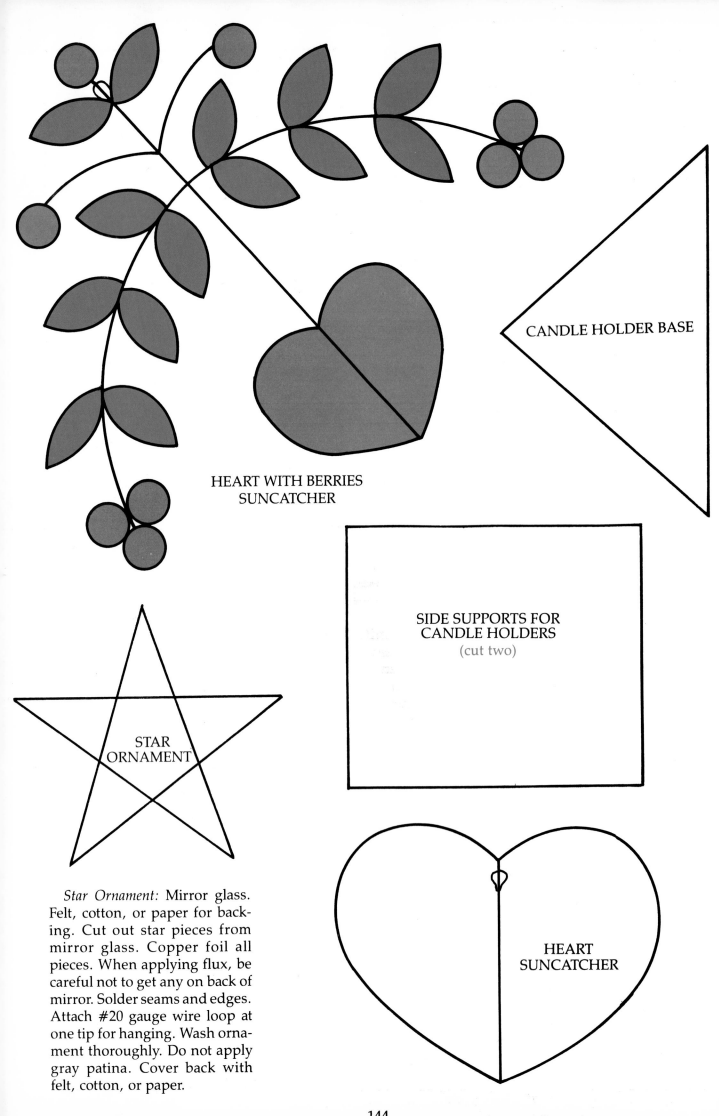

CANDLE HOLDER BASE

HEART WITH BERRIES
SUNCATCHER

SIDE SUPPORTS FOR
CANDLE HOLDERS
(cut two)

STAR
ORNAMENT

HEART
SUNCATCHER

Star Ornament: Mirror glass. Felt, cotton, or paper for backing. Cut out star pieces from mirror glass. Copper foil all pieces. When applying flux, be careful not to get any on back of mirror. Solder seams and edges. Attach #20 gauge wire loop at one tip for hanging. Wash ornament thoroughly. Do not apply gray patina. Cover back with felt, cotton, or paper.

144

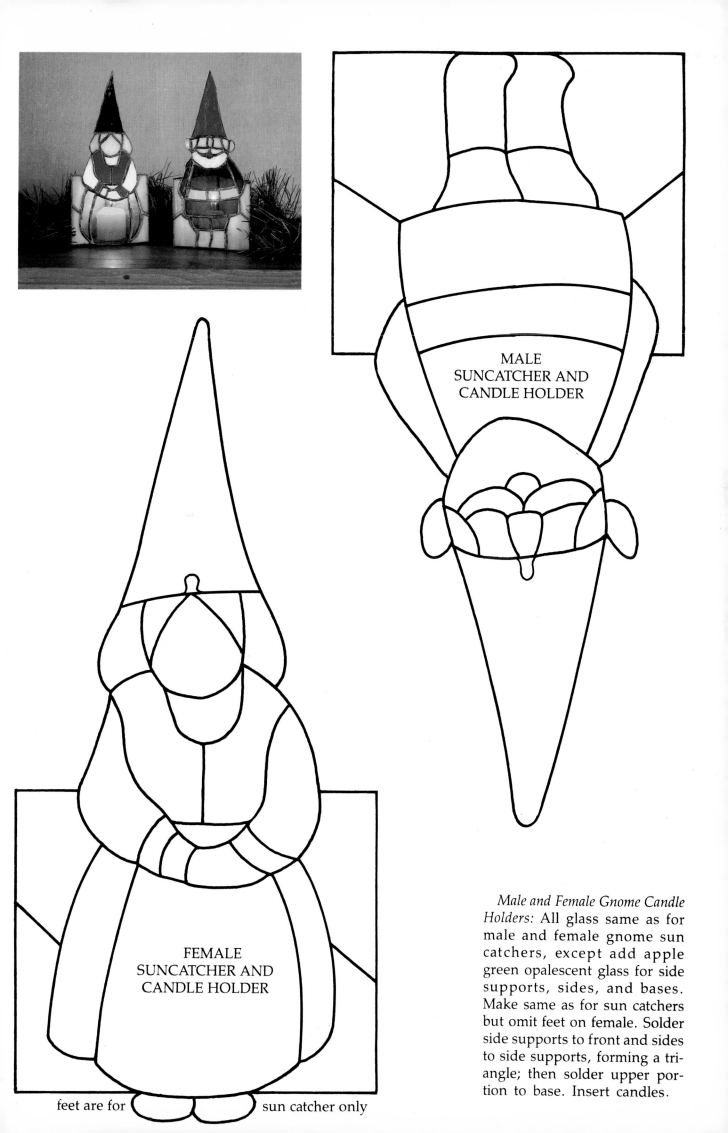

MALE
SUNCATCHER AND
CANDLE HOLDER

FEMALE
SUNCATCHER AND
CANDLE HOLDER

feet are for   sun catcher only

Male and Female Gnome Candle Holders: All glass same as for male and female gnome sun catchers, except add apple green opalescent glass for side supports, sides, and bases. Make same as for sun catchers but omit feet on female. Solder side supports to front and sides to side supports, forming a triangle; then solder upper portion to base. Insert candles.

Silver Pouch

SKILL LEVEL: Intermediate

MATERIALS: White/red calico, 45″ wide, ⅝ yard. Co-ordinating extra-wide double-fold bias seam tape, 2 yards. Scrap red polka dot cotton fabric. White button. Batting. Fiberfill.

DIRECTIONS: Cut two 20″ squares from white/red calico; cut two 20″ squares from batting. Insert batting between squares of calico; baste together with raw edges even. Cut 5″ length of bias seam tape for loop; sew long edges together, then sew ends to one corner of square with raw edges even. Sandwich all raw edges of padded square with bias seam tape, easing tape around corners; slip-stitch tape to calico on front and back overlapping ends.

Position square on work surface with loop at top; fold corner of square opposite loop 5″ toward center; pin in place. Fold adjacent corners toward pinned corner so edges are flush; pin. Tack corners together at center. Trace pattern and use to cut two hearts from red polka dot fabric; sew together with right sides facing and raw edges even, leaving opening for turning; clip curves and turn to right side. Stuff heart with fiberfill; slip-stitch opening closed. Slip-stitch heart over tacked corners of square. Attach button to square just below heart. Button pouch closed with loop.

ADAPTATION: Use as lingerie bag or correspondence keeper.

HEART
PATTERN

Female Gnome Tea Cozy

Note: Before beginning, read General Directions for Soft Sculpture Head on page 18; for Painting on Fabric on page 20; and for Embroidery on page 18.

SKILL LEVEL: Advanced

MATERIALS: *For Body:* Medium-weight muslin, 45″ wide, 1⅓ yards. Fiberfill. White fake fur with at least 1½″ nap, large piece. Thread. Acrylic paint: white, red, yellow, blue, steel gray, burnt sienna. Brown felt-tipped fine line marking pen. Ruler. White glue. Graphite paper. *For Clothes:* White fabric, 45″ wide: sheer, ¼ yard; cotton, 1⅛ yards. Cotton fabric, 36″ wide: red, ¼ yard; green, ⅔ yard. Lace trim, 1″ wide, 1¼ yards. White buttons: 3 small heart-shaped, ¾″ diameter. White, green, red thread. White and hunter green double-fold bias seam tape. Six-strand embroidery floss, one skein each color listed in *Color Key.* Five hooks and eyes.

DIRECTIONS: Enlarge and trace all patterns. Cut a 20″-diameter circle from muslin for head. Use patterns to cut out nose from muslin, two wig halves from white fake fur, cap from gray felt. Complete head and make cap following directions on page 20.

Use pattern to cut four arms from muslin. Sew two pairs of arms together with raw edges even, assembling pieces so you have a right and left arm, leaving tops open for turning. Turn to right side; stuff hand and lower arm firmly with fiberfill, leaving 2″ lightly stuffed below open end. Mark lines for fingers on each hand; machine-quilt along lines. Paint arms flesh (*see Body Diagram*).

Cut two 11½ x 8″ pieces from muslin for torso. Sew 8″ edges together, making a tube; turn to right side. Hand-baste around raw edges at both ends; pull

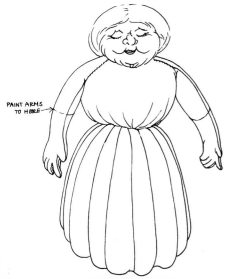

PAINT ARMS
TO HERE →

basting tight at one end (bottom); push raw edges inside and tie off. Pull basting at other end slightly, then fill pouch with fiberfill to medium firmness. Insert neck into opening so face is centered between side seams, then pull and tie off basting, enclosing fiberfill and raw edges. Slip-stitch head securely in place. Slip-stitch arms to sides, making sure thumbs face front.

For bra, cut 8 x 6½" piece from muslin; sew long edges to-

gether to form tube. Turn to right side; hand-baste top to bottom across center, dividing tube into two equal halves. Pull basting thread to gather center to 2" width; tie off. Stuff each half firmly with fiberfill. Fold raw edges to one side, enclosing fiberfill; slip-stitch to secure. Slip-stitch bra to front of bosom along each side edge.

For lower body section, cut 35½ x 24" piece from muslin. Fold in half crosswise, matching 35½" edges. Machine-baste ¼"

147

away from each side (12") edge to secure. Using ruler and pencil, draw parallel lines between basted lines, each spaced 2½" apart, making 14 sections; sew along each marked line, backstitching at top and bottom to reinforce. Sew side edges together, making a tube. With folded edge at bottom, begin stuffing each channel with fiberfill, forcing stuffing to bottom. Stuff lower 6" so all channels are firm but relatively flat, then stuff upper 6" of alternate channels very firmly so channels become rounded. Stuff upper 5" of all other channels in same manner, leaving 1" unstuffed at tops of these channels; body should take on a bell-shape. Hand-baste across upper edge, making two rows of stitching. Pull basting, gathering top tightly; push raw edges into bell and tie off basting. To cover raw edges on inside, cut circle from muslin and glue over raw edges. Slip-stitch bottom of torso securely to top of bell-shaped lower body.

Slip: Cut a 40 x 9" piece from sheer white fabric. Press one long edge ¼" to wrong side for hem. Overlap unfinished edge of lace trim over pressed edge; sew in place, securing lace and hem. Starting at bottom (lace edge), with right sides facing and raw edges even, sew short edges of strip together for 5" for back seam; press unsewn raw edges ¼" to wrong side and sew in place. Hand-baste around top of slip and gather to fit waist of gnome. Cut 30"-length of double-fold bias seam tape; center over gathered edge of slip. Topstitch tape to slip, covering gathered edges, and continue to topstitch excess tape, which will become ties.

Blouse: Use patterns to cut one blouse front (placing pattern on fold of fabric), two blouse backs (do not place pattern on fold of fabric), and two sleeves from white fabric. Use patterns to cut one collar and two cuffs from red fabric. With right sides facing and raw edges

even on back pieces, sew center back seam of blouse up to dot; press raw edges from dot to opening ¼" to wrong side and sew in place. Sew blouse front to blouse back at sides and shoulders. Baste around neck edge and gather. Press seam allowance on collar ¼" to wrong side as indicated. Pin neck edge of blouse to collar with right sides facing and raw edges even, starting at center back on right side and ending at marked line on left side, forming an extension; sew together, adjusting gathers. Remove basting. Fold collar in half with right sides facing; sew right side edge, continuing to center back seam in straight line. Sew left side edge of collar, turning stitching sharply at corner. Trim seams, clipping corners. Turn collar to right side; slip-stitch pressed edge to blouse along seamline, covering raw edges. Make buttonhole on collar extension; attach heart-shaped button on opposite side at X. Sew each sleeve seam from underarm to large dot; press raw edges from dot to edge of sleeve ¼" to wrong side and sew.

Press seam allowance on each cuff ¼" to wrong side as indicated. Baste around bottom of each sleeve and gather; sew sleeve to cuff with right sides facing and raw edges even. Fold each cuff in half with right sides facing; sew each side edge. Turn cuffs to right side; slip-stitch pressed edge of each cuff to sleeve, covering raw edges. Overlap edges of cuffs; tack and attach heart-shaped button at marked X's. Baste sleeve caps between dots and gather. With right sides facing and raw edges even, pin sleeves into armholes, easing as necessary. Sew sleeves to blouse. Turn bottom of blouse under along marked line and hem.

Skirt: Use pattern to cut one waistband and two 30 x 11" skirts from green fabric. Sew short edges of skirt pieces together, making one large circle of fabric, and leaving 4" opening along

one seam (top). Fold unsewn seam allowance ¼" to wrong side and sew in place. Fold bottom edge of skirt under ½", then 1¼"; press and hem. Press one long edge of waistband ¼" to wrong side. Baste top edge of skirt and gather; with right sides facing and raw edges even, sew waistband to skirt. Remove basting. Fold waistband in half with right sides facing, and sew each side edge; turn to right side. Slip-stitch pressed edge of waistband to skirt. Make a buttonhole at one end; attach three buttons to waistband, one opposite buttonhole and one at each X for attaching apron to skirt.

Apron: Use patterns to cut one apron and one waistband from white fabric. Transfer embroidery design to apron. Following directions on page 18 embroider border design in lazy daisy stitch using three strands of red floss in needle. Turn hem to wrong side along fold line; press and baste in place. Using red thread, machine-embroider areas between parallel lines using zigzag satin stitch; embroidery will secure hem. Trim raw edges of hem if necessary when embroidery is completed, then remove basting. Press raw edge of waistband ¼" to wrong side of fabric. Baste and gather top edge of apron and sew to waistband between dots. Remove basting. Fold waistband in half with right sides facing and sew each corner from dot to fold; turn to right side. Slip-stitch pressed edge of waistband to apron. Make buttonhole at each end of waistband. Attach apron to buttons on skirt.

Kerchief: Use pattern to cut two kerchief pieces from white fabric. Transfer embroidery design to one piece. Following directions on page 18, embroider all dots with French knots; embroider curved interior lines with chain stitch, using three strands of red floss in needle. With right sides facing and raw edges even, sew kerchief pieces

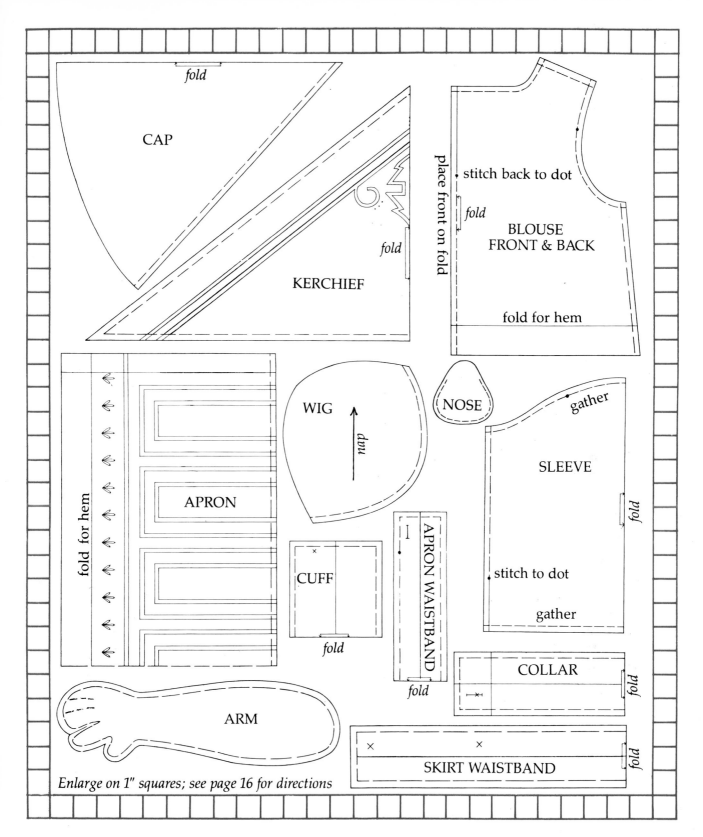

CAP

fold

KERCHIEF

fold

fold

place front on fold

stitch back to dot

BLOUSE
FRONT & BACK

fold

fold for hem

WIG

nap

NOSE

gather

SLEEVE

fold

stitch to dot

gather

APRON

fold for hem

CUFF

fold

APRON WAISTBAND

fold

COLLAR

fold

ARM

SKIRT WAISTBAND

fold

Enlarge on 1" squares; see page 16 for directions

TEA COZY

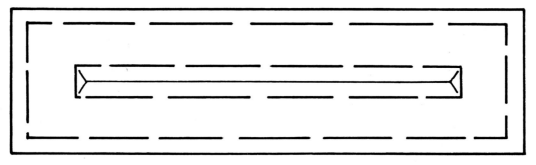

VEST FACING

149

together around all edges, leaving opening for turning. Turn to right side and press; slip-stitch opening closed. Using red thread, machine-embroider border lines with close zigzag satin stitch.

Vest: Use pattern to mark one vest back and two vest fronts on red fabric, reversing pattern to mark second vest front; do not cut out. Transfer embroidery design to right side of each piece. Following directions on page 18 and using three strands of floss in needle, embroider pieces (except for buttonhole stitches around opening on vest fronts), following *Color Key* and *Stitch Key* as well as colors on pattern; for areas labeled only with a *Stitch Key*, work design in that color (it will be indicated on *Color Key* without a number). Use vest facing pattern to cut two facings from red fabric. Center each facing carefully over line for opening on vest front; sew together with right sides facing, turning stitching sharply at corners. Cut through center of sewn area from top to bottom; cut fabric to each corner at an angle as shown on facing. Turn facing through opening to wrong side; press and baste in place. Work buttonhole stitch around opening; remove basting. Steam-press embroidery face down on padded surface. Cut out pieces; with right sides facing and raw edges even, sew together at sides and shoulders.

For vest lining, use patterns to cut one vest back and two

vest fronts from white fabric; sew together with raw edges even at sides and shoulders. With wrong sides facing, baste white lining to embroidered vest close to all raw edges. Sew hunter green double-fold bias seam tape over raw edges of vest around each armhole and all outer edges. Attach five hooks and eyes, spaced evenly, along center front opening.

COLOR KEY FOR TEA COZY				
1 White	2 Pink	Yellow	3 Orange	4 Light blue
Medium blue		5 Navy blue	6 Chartreuse	Apple green
	7 Hunter green		8 Lavender	

STITCH KEY		
A Chain Stitch	B Outline Stitch	C Satin Stitch
D Lazy Daisy Stitch	F French Knot	G Buttonhole Stitch
	H Straight Stitch	

Hanging Heart

SKILL LEVEL: Elementary

MATERIALS: Large scrap red polka dot fabric. Kelly green grosgrain ribbon, ⅜" wide, ½ yard. Fiberfill.

DIRECTIONS: Trace pattern and use to cut two hearts from red polka dot fabric. Sew together with right sides facing and raw edges even, leaving opening for turning; clip curves. Turn to right side; stuff firmly with fiberfill. Fold raw edges to inside and slip-stitch opening closed.

Cut three 6"-lengths of ribbon; slip-stitch ends of two together. Wrap one end of third length of ribbon around each circle at center; tack in place, fashioning two bows. Slip-stitch one bow to center top of heart; hang from other bow.

ADAPTATION: Make sachet using your favorite potpourri to stuff heart.

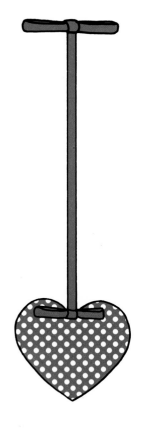

HANGING HEART PATTERN

Gnome Prints

Cut out and use where indicated
or wherever you choose

for gingerbread farmhouse, p. 46

window for gingerbread farmhouse, p. 46

for papered   cookies, p. 41

for gnome puzzle, p. 99

for gift tags, p. 99

for gnome puzzle, p. 99

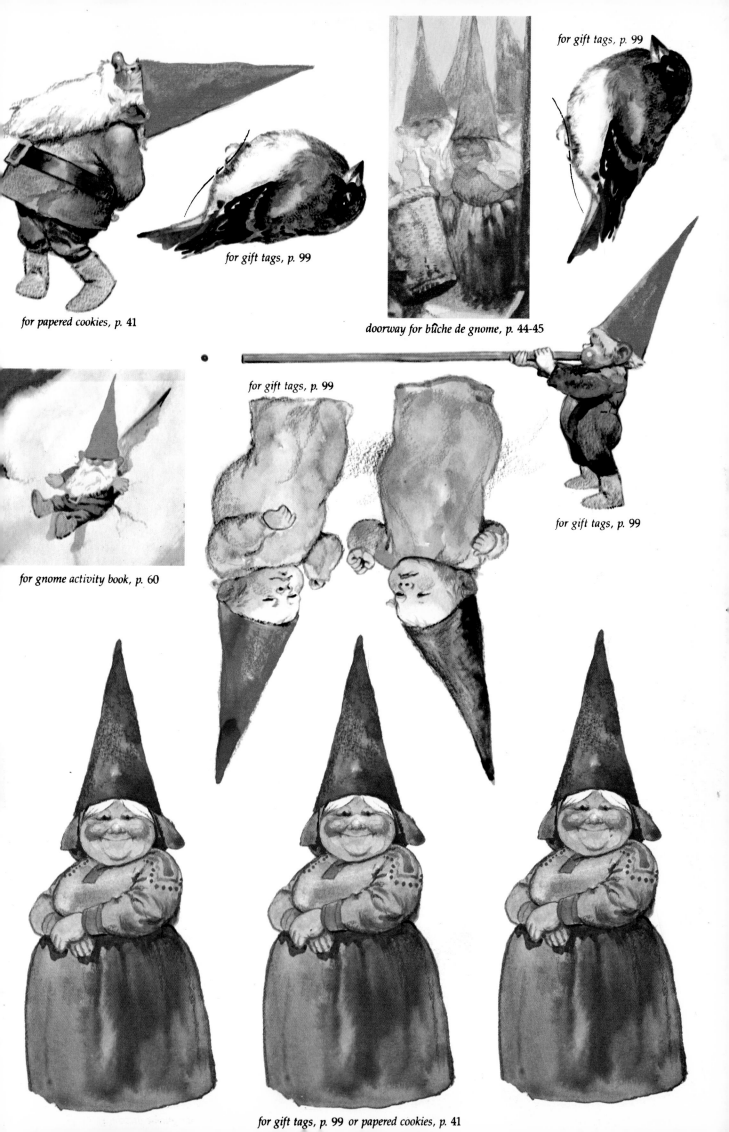

for papered cookies, p. 41

for gift tags, p. 99

doorway for bûche de gnome, p. 44-45

for gift tags, p. 99

for gift tags, p. 99

for gnome activity book, p. 60

for gift tags, p. 99

for gift tags, p. 99 or papered cookies, p. 41

handle for soap box, p. 93

decoration for soap, p. 93

for papered cookies, p. 41

for gift tags, p. 99
or papered cookies, p. 41

Index

Guide to the Crafts
By Technique
And Skill Level

E = *Elementary*

I = *Intermediate*

A = *Advanced*